PARANORMAL
COTSWOLDS

PARANORMAL COTSWOLDS

ANTHONY POULTON—SMITH

AMBERLEY

First published 2009

Amberley Publishing
Cirencester Road, Chalford,
Stroud, Gloucestershire, GL6 8PE

www.amberley-books.com

British Library Cataloguing in Publication Data.
A catalogue record for this book is available from the British Library.

ISBN 978 1 84868 170 5

Typesetting and origination by Amberley Publishing
Printed in Great Britain

CONTENTS

INTRODUCTION

During 2007 I had the opportunity to research a book on ghosts. My personal experience in the supernatural is limited to just a split second. Indeed so brief was the experience that I have yet to be convinced of the existence of ghosts.

Having embarked on a year-long search for ghosts around the Cotswolds I still have an open mind. However, I am certain that those who related their experiences fervently believe what they saw could not be explained by anything other than a ghost. During my search I found many stories, some had been told many times and yet were a part of the history and tradition of the area and simply could not be omitted. Others had never appeared in print before, even though few of these were contemporary.

Even if I have yet to be convinced of their existence, I admit to having become fascinated by the stories. Not only what happened but to whom, the people who relate them. While the places themselves have allowed me to visit everything from castles and stately homes to the latest semi-detached or terraced council house.

Thus as soon as I had sampled the tales of the supernatural I was anxious to continue in a different region and soon turned my attention to the Cotswolds. Encompassing parts of Oxfordshire, Gloucestershire, Warwickshire and Wiltshire there are a wealth of tales awaiting us on the following pages. Indeed just about every likely ghostly figure I can think of is covered – the aristocrat and the lowliest servant, the elderly man or woman to the youngest child, the most faithful pet and the wildest animal.

It is interesting to note how many of these sightings are at public houses. Whether this is indicative of the strength of the beer, or possibly the amount consumed, is for the reader to decide for themselves. There also seems to be a rather substantial number of churchmen, considerably more than would be expected considering the proportion of religious figures within the community.

There are tales of those who were horrified by their experiences, although few of the manifestations could be considered malevolent. Most of the people I met were simply unable to offer any other explanation for what they had seen, although there were a few who still remained sceptical despite their experiences. Some were indifferent to their uninvited visitors, others even amused by what they had encountered. To all who have contributed, even in the smallest way, I give my thanks. Special thanks goes to the staff of every library, the Gloucestershire Record Office, Holt Hotel, Haunting Breaks, and Cotswold Wildlife Park.

No matter what these encounters are, whether tricks of the light or the mind, or misinterpretations of what was thought to have been seen, felt or heard is not relevant here. This book is intended solely to record the narratives, both the traditional and the new which appear for the first time in print.

It is for the reader to make up their own mind in each case.

CHAPTER 1

BAMPTON

MRS WHITTAKER

A tale of heartache from the manor house in Bampton. The cause of the heartache was Mr Whittaker, who fell for a servant girl working in the village. Poor Mrs Whittaker, born today she would have sued for divorce and taken her unfaithful husband for every penny she could. In reality she stayed by his side and was said to have died from a broken heart at an early age.

For some reason, in this area whenever a haunting is suspected the bodies are laid in a nearby pond, and the lady of the house was no exception. However, her spirit in death was clearly stronger than in life for she returned to haunt the home where she was so unhappy during her final years. None of the reports of her appearances in the manor house at this time describe anything other than her presence. Even from the grave she remained quite forgiving and kindly in her treatment of her former husband.

An unexpected turn came about when the pond dried up. This was given as one reason why her spirit was so restless. In order to quieten her she was subjected to the extraordinary ignominy of being sealed in a barrel of the strongest ale and then walled up in the cellar of her former home. While it is believed that there was a second funeral ceremony for the poor lady, this still seems a little extreme considering she wasn't guilty of anything.

There is a documented record of her odd casket still being there at the end of the nineteenth century. Indeed there is no reason to suppose it is not still contained within the walls of the cellar, although it remains unknown whether the poor woman still haunts the place.

BIRDLIP

WEST TUMP LONG BARROW

A Neolithic mound dating from four or even five thousand years ago. Inside there were different chambers. To the south, a passageway led to a chamber lined with the skeletons of many individuals, all men. Here is a stone, a semi-circular block upon which was found the remains of a single female and, alongside her, the remains of a child.

One weekend, walkers were enjoying the delights of the countryside when a most unusual sight was seen by one of them. Passing the tomb she had seen so often and with which she was so familiar, it came as no surprise to see four people standing on top of it. However, on closer inspection these were no twentieth-century hikers, these were four men who would not have looked out of place when the tomb was first constructed. Wearing short breeches or skirts of leather or coarse cloth, their chests were bare and bronzed, their hair wild and naturally curly, while each was holding a spear. The image lasted for several moments before fading.

Was this a flashback to when four warriors lamented the passing of their fellow men or, more poignantly, were they mourning the passing of a woman and child who had been important members of the family of chieftains?

BISLEY

MONEY TUMP

A burial mound or long barrow which still stands almost two metres high and measures over sixty-five metres in circumference. It is at least 3,000 years old and may well be older. One traditional tale states there is a hidden treasure trove just awaiting discovery here; however, the area has been surveyed several times using increasingly advanced geophysics mapping techniques and nothing has ever been found. Indeed the modern sensory methods are so sensitive they would even have found potential sites where the mound had been robbed, had this been the case, and nothing has been found. This story almost certainly comes from the name Money Tump, but this is simply the name of the place and has nothing to do with cash, coin or secret cache.

These Neolithic burial mounds are often associated with spiritual activities and Money Tump was no exception. During the twentieth century two people passing here were astounded to see a group of phantoms standing on top of the mound without a single head between them. The view was momentary from the vehicle, so perhaps the men had their heads bowed in prayer or reverence to the dead. If so, was this perhaps the memory of an ancient burial, when the bones of a chieftain or a close member of his family were entombed here for posterity?

BOURTON ON THE WATER

OLD MANSE HOTEL

One of the most rewarding aspects when travelling and researching ghost stories is to find one which has a name. This may be in the form of a nickname, making the apparition seem personable, even friendly and welcomed. Alternatively this could be a known (or should that be reputed?) individual said to be in residence. It seems that here we have a visit from someone who could fit in either or even both categories. This then is the story of George and room thirteen.

This story was told by Amber, whose bedroom is on the relevant floor of the hotel, and with great assistance from Ben, a barman who has worked at the premises for much longer and was better informed on the question of George and his activities.

In 1748 this building was opened as a Baptist Church. The only sign of this today is the room which remembers the name of the former church: named after the dedication of the church it is clearly marked the Bedome Suite. During its time as a church it had a number of rooms, including one on the upper floor which was marked as No. 13.

Old Manse Hotel, Bourton-on-the-Water.

Luck, either good or bad, does not seem to have played any part in this story, hence the number thirteen cannot be blamed.

It was said that in this room, a guest named George hanged himself. Why he chose suicide, and why here, have never been understood, for he is said to have left no note, had not confided in anyone and, while not entirely unknown in the area, could not be considered a local man. Even an approximate date of this tragic event is unknown. Such matters were rarely recorded then as it was the job of the Church to record internments or funerals and suicides were denied a burial in consecrated ground for many years. This suicide had nothing to do with the church closing as it continued to be a place of worship until 1938.

The building opened as a hotel in 1963. Upstairs are the rooms which are available to staff and paying guests alike. Making our way along the corridors we pass the numbered doors and yet, despite the tales which have been passed down, there is no number thirteen on any door. This room is said to have disappeared and we have no way of knowing how the building has changed for plans of the original building are no longer available.

Meanwhile, George continues to make his presence felt. He is sensed rather than seen, a presence, a feeling of being watched or stood over has unnerved many a newcomer. Yet his presence, while uncomfortable, has never been considered aggressive or threatening. Indeed whenever a change of staff or a reorganisation of the furniture rouses the interest of the ghostly resident, Amber's advice was simply to reassure him with a quietly spoken: 'It's OK George, I know you're here and everything is fine'.

THE KINGSBRIDGE

A former employee at this old pub reported the place to be haunted by a Lord Tarquin. Speaking to the manager he said he had never heard of anything personally and, having asked around the oldest regulars, could not find any word of Tarquin or anyone else. However, it was interesting to note than when I first contacted the place I spoke to Jonathan, a barman who has only worked there for a comparatively short time and had never heard of any haunting. Yet he was quite relieved to hear of my lead because he had 'Always thought there was something hanging about this place'.

For the time being the question remains unanswered.

BROADWAY

Dormy House Hotel

A ghostly lady has been seen in and around that part of the hotel used as the conference centre. Several cleaners and service staff have seen her, as has one guest. She is described as a woman of around fifty years of age, wearing a pale coloured shawl. Her appearances, whilst brief, are always of her facing toward and walking off to the right of the observer, which means her right arm is closest. This is important, for this is the only part of her which seems solid, the rest of her is diffuse even faded. Recently she was seen by a night porter seated in a rocking chair, again with her right-hand side closest to the witness.

Speaking to the administration staff of the conference centre, one senses that they are more concerned for the apparition than for themselves. There is a concern, a sadness when she is mentioned, for it is rumoured the hotel is located on the site of a former burial ground. However, this is often given as the reason for unexplained phenomena when there is no evidence to prove it. Furthermore, even if the burial ground theory is correct, the woman's appearance would suggest she is from a more recent era than any forgotten burial site.

BURFORD

The Brown Monk

Since the Second World War nuns of a Roman Catholic order have resided at the ancient priory. After its days as a priory, and before the arrival of the sisters, it was a private residence. The owner at the time was subjected to many hauntings, eventually disposing of it to a religious order believing this was the only way of putting the little brown monk's mind to rest.

However, despite the good intentions of this quite plausible theory, the inmates could still hear a bell ringing at two in the morning. It was thought to be an echo of the bell that called the monks to prayer at the priory at this very time during the medieval period. Furthermore, the singing of a choir is heard at various times of the day.

There are other signs of the priory's past. The visitor is known as 'the monk', a small figure wearing a brown habit. He has been seen mainly in the area used as the chapel, although he does appear elsewhere. This diminutive figure pays no attention to anyone, seemingly blissfully unaware of the presence of anyone in the modern world.

He is not the only ghost of the priory. The rectory is also haunted by an apparition which reveals his coming by a feeling of deepening gloom. Items are heard being thrown around a room which is no longer used and, on later inspection, appears untouched. Nothing has ever been seen of this individual, only heard, and it may be that this is the same figure as has been seen in the grounds. He is described as a surly individual carrying an old gun. Whenever and whatever he encounters is completely ignored and he walks straight through anything in his way. His appearance seems to be that of a gamekeeper. However, he may be a poacher for they proverbially make the best gamekeepers.

Throughout the site people have heard inexplicable sounds – footsteps along an empty corridor, doors opening and closing of their own volition, and knocks on the outer door that have announced the arrival of an unseen visitor.

SIR LAURENCE TANFIELD

A man whose career encompassed lawyer, politician and landholder: a prominent figure in the country between 1583 and 1625. Born around 1551, his earlier years are something of a mystery but we do know he was admitted to the bar of the Inner Temple in 1569 and was extremely successful, enabling him to purchase an estate at Burford in 1583 and later lands at Great Tew. Burford Priory was built at his behest on his lands where a mental hospital had previously stood.

In 1584 he entered parliament as MP for New Woodstock, twenty years later he was returned for the county of Oxford and knighted by James I. The king had been a guest of Tanfield's *en route* to London in the autumn of 1603 and clearly enjoyed an excellent rapport with Tanfield. In 1607 Sir Laurence was Chief Baron of the Exchequer, a position he held until his death.

However, while his professional career was undoubtedly successful, in Burford and Great Tew the inhabitants had a revealing story to tell. By 1617 as Lord of the Manor of Burford, he and his wife were involved in a number of disputes with both the inhabitants and the local administration. Indeed the reputation of Lord and Lady Tanfield as greedy and corrupt remains a part of Burford folklore. Having stripped Burford church of every valuable, purportedly to be in settlement of a dispute with the then vicar, although the circumstances regarding the dispute and the supposed agreement are suspicious, the people thereafter saw him as 'the very devil among us'. So reviled was he that the people of Burford celebrated his death by burning an effigy of Lord Tanfield around the anniversary each and every year and continued to do so for over 200 years.

It was probably unwise for his widow, who herself died three years later, to return to the church of St Catherine's and erect a quite astonishingly outlandish monument to her husband, which also allowed for room for her when her time came. The craftsmanship of the sculpture is unquestionable, the design ugly and clearly not the conception of anyone with the talents to produce such work but undoubtedly produced exactly to the orders of the widow. However, perhaps the sculptors, embarrassed by the work they had probably been paid an exceptional sum of money to produce, made their own comment on the memorial. Bending down to look underneath the carving one will see a frail skeleton, invisible to the casual observer and unlikely to have been part of the widow's design. Is it suggesting that, neither money nor power can save anyone from the inevitability of death.

Yet the story does not end there, for Sir Laurence is still said to be about today. He has been seen driving a coach pulled by four impossibly black horses in a number of places around his former estates. It is claimed that each and every one of these witnesses suffered bad luck following the sighting of the phantom coach and its notorious driver, although how the vision of the coach and horses is identified with Sir Laurence is unclear.

Furthermore it has been suggested that the skeletal carving beneath the sculpture was not created by mortal hand but a warning added by the lord of the manor announcing his return to this world after his wife's death.

The gruesome reminder of the Tanfield mortality.

THE BROWN NUN

After the end of the Second World War, when life was beginning to return to normal and potential university students emerged, tutors and lecturers were required. This was how Professor Humphrey arrived at Oxford in 1948. The man was not unfamiliar with the area, indeed his sister was at Burford Priory and he took the first chance he could to visit her.

When he arrived he was shown into a small room, the fire burned brightly and warmed the otherwise spartan interior. He waited a few moments gazing into the flames, when the door opened and a nun walked in. She ignored the professor completely and walked up to the fire, bracing herself with her forearm on the mantelpiece and leaning across the radiating heat. The professor thought she was deep in prayer or meditation and chose not to interrupt her. Shortly afterwards she stood upright and left the room, without acknowledging the professor.

Mere moments afterwards another nun entered and this time it was the sister of Professor Humphrey. After a while the professor asked his sister about the differing colours of the nuns' habits, why did she wear a grey habit when others wore brown. His sister was perplexed and informed her brother that all the nuns wore grey whether they be the leader of the order or the newest junior member. She knew nothing of anyone wearing brown and had not seen the other nun leave the room as she had approached.

When he returned to Oxford he mentioned this oddity to a colleague, who just happened to be working in the history department and who was fully aware the nuns of Burford only wore grey. A few weeks later the man met up with Professor Humphrey in the street. As with most historians he had been bothered by the inaccuracies of the colour of the habits and had undertaken a little research. He had discovered that, for a few short years in the middle of the fifteenth century, the nuns had belonged to a group known as the Poor Clares. These nuns wore habits of a brown cloth.

COTSWOLD WILDLIFE PARK

In 1970, two miles south of Burford at Bradwell Grove, the wildlife park threw open its gates to visitors for the first time. Today, almost forty years later, it is still a delight to see the animals roaming the grounds and the sight of a grazing rhino just feet away has been a lasting memory for the author.

However, it is not the grounds but the Victorian manor house that demands our attention, for this is where John and Jean Boxall came to live in 1994 and where they were to serve as catering managers for the next eight years. The orangery and lower floors of the old house still serve as restaurant and bar, while the upper floors provide living accommodation for some of the staff.

Having settled in they heard from others of the odd events that had been reported there over the years, so it came as no great shock when they started having their own experiences. What was unnerving at first became less unsettling in later years. In the flat they were soon quite accustomed to the sensation of young children cuddling up against them as they sat on the sofa in the evenings. The rocking horse, part of the furniture they kept for their own grandchildren, was another target for the unseen children. It was seen to move as if being ridden when nobody was around. The living room door, a heavy, old wooden design, was known to open on its own and on more than one occasion a mist had been seen in the bathroom. Mrs Boxall had once ordered it out, but had had to resort to walking through it, and had also seen the diffuse image of a person formed by the cloud.

A predecessor, who was still working there but no longer in residence, reported how he had often found things moved in this particular flat. The furniture would be rearranged, his keys or tobacco tin changed places without warning. Nothing malevolent was ever sensed and nothing threatening, but these occurrences were worrying nevertheless. A keeper who lived in the neighbouring flat recounted his own identical experience when Mr Boxall told him of how he had woken in the night to feel a pressure bearing down upon him. Nothing could be felt touching him, just a heavy weight bearing down and pinning him to the bed.

During their early days duties included catering for other sites within the group. Once the evening ran very late and Mr Boxall had to telephone his wife to say he would not be home that evening. She pleaded and implored him to hurry for she was not happy on her own in their flat, but he could not leave the job. The next morning he drove home with a bunch of flowers on the passenger seat by way of apology for his enforced absence, only to be made to promise he would never again leave her on her own in the premises overnight. Some time later, when his wife was away from home for a few nights, Mr Boxall admits to being very uneasy by himself in the flat and resorted to sleeping on the sofa and with the light on!

To gain access to the flats meant a walk up the stairs and on an occasion when the poor man had suffered from a badly broken ankle, a quite new phenomenon revealed itself. He was ascending the steps in the accepted reverse seating position when a bell rang. This was not the doorbell but an old service bell used to summon the household staff. Such devices were based on a manual pull and it was a simple task of following the attached wire or chord to ascertain who had activated the bell. Fearing intruders, several of the resident staff traced it to a padlocked room which had clearly not been opened for many years. A later look at the plans showed it to have been the housekeeper's service bell, but no explanation as to why it had sounded could be found.

Outside the manor house today is a modern surface but in earlier years all was quite different. In the evenings, when staff can gaze out across the park and watch the animals continuing to graze in the moonlight, sounds have been heard coming from below.

Almost as if transported back in time, one can hear the sound of the horses' hooves and the wheels of the coach crossing the old cobblestones of the former courtyard as it draws up to the house.

However, their most unnerving experience came when problems had been encountered with a walk-in freezer. Temperatures would fluctuate without warning and, having sent for the engineers, they were warned to keep an eye on the thermometer for the first few days. Later that same day they locked up the restaurant for the day and headed off upstairs for their evening meal. Settling down the peace was disturbed by the sound of the restaurant's alarm system and they went to investigate. A walking stick was removed from the boot of the car, should there be a need to defend themselves, and after disarming the system they entered the building. There was nobody there and the other door was still locked and no signs of entry. They took the opportunity to check on the recently repaired freezer and to wash out a few tea towels for the next day. Standing within reach of one another they both felt a simultaneous frosty chill pass by, almost as if they had walked into the freezer which was still closed quite firmly.

Next morning the morning routine was identical, and the bar and till were left to the last. When Mrs Boxall called out to her husband and asked him if he had seen the bar he replied he had not until he walked through the door and saw a most inexplicable sight. Every cushion on the seats had been scattered around the edges of the room and glasses from behind the bar were strewn everywhere, although there was not a crack, chip or break to be found on a single one. Turning to the barmaid Mr Boxall asked her if she would tidy up and, although very reluctant at first, she eventually relented. Moments later she ran from the room and told how she had seen more glasses flying through the air from behind the bar almost as if in slow motion. The barmaid left her job that very moment.

So regular were the events which, quite understandably, bothered those who were resident here, that the owner of the Cotswold Wildlife Park offered to organise an exorcism in an attempt to end the worries. However, the Boxalls and other members of staff turned down the opportunity for fear of angering the resident ghost or ghosts. There was no sense of malevolence and they could see no sense in disturbing them further.

Cotswold Wildlife Park, taken the morning after the disturbing paranormal activites.

CHAPTER 2

CHALFORD

GYPSY LANE

During the seventeenth century a young girl was working for a rich farmer as a maid. Unknown to her employer, she was head-over-heels in love with his son and heir and the couple had embarked on a very passionate affair. In order to keep their liaisons secret from the farmer she always arranged to meet her beau at a stile in the corner of the field adjoining Gypsy Lane.

One must assume it was here where she met her love one day and told him the news that she was with child. Any joy she may have felt at motherhood, and maybe even pride, soon evaporated, for her lover immediately rejected her, choosing to avoid the displeasure of his father and safeguarding his inheritance by ending their love affair that day. Within a matter of hours the girl, her future plans in tatters, had taken her own life and was found hanging from the rafters of a barn.

During the Second World War the RAF were stationed near here and groups of them would habitually use Gypsy Lane to reach the pub at the bottom of Cowcombe Hill. On the way they would pass this stile and several reported seeing a pretty young woman seated there, staring into the distance and seemingly awaiting someone. Her dress seemed out-dated, belonging to a much earlier age. Being young, hot-blooded males away from home several of them, somewhat predictably, approached the young lady and spoke to her. It was at this moment that the young lady, of apparent flesh and blood, promptly vanished.

Men and women who were as brave as any to take on the enemy at a moment's notice changed their local and avoided Gypsy Lane entirely.

CONTEMPORARY GYPSY LANE

With the twenty-first century still in its infancy, a visitor to this area had spent much of the day in the area making arrangements to find a house and move here. Not being fully aware of the place, he was unsure where he could find an all-night garage in order to fill up his somewhat depleted petrol tank.

Thus, when he found himself in Gypsy Lane he was not exactly lost but just not sure what he would find there. What he did see has left a lasting impression on him. Reaching the glider club he realised he was unlikely to discover any fuel in this direction and so pulled in to a lay-by opposite what had been the old RAF airfield during the Second World War in order to turn the car around and retrace his path.

The road is not very wide here and the car was only moving slowly as he turned, but still the headlights swung across an astonishing scene rather abruptly. The lights picked out an old-fashioned gypsy caravan with its curved roof and colours apparent even in the darkness. The horse was unhitched and grazing, while an elderly woman in dated clothing (he guessed the Victorian era) was chopping wood. There was no light for her to see what she was doing, if there had been he would have noticed before he turned the car around.

Whilst he knew the area – he had found his bearings from the glider club – he was not aware of the name of the road. Indeed, it was not until several weeks later that he discovered he had been in Gypsy Lane and wondered if there was some connection. It is most likely that the name referred to a former resident. However, whether they had had the ability to chop wood in complete darkness is not recorded.

CHARLBURY

CORNBURY PARK

One of the very few stories which, if the identity of the apparition is correct, can be traced to a single day. The estate at Cornbury was created as a royal hunting park, ostensibly for deer, and resulted in the annexing of part of the adjacent Wychwood Forest. This woodland survives as part of some of the most ancient forests still to be seen in England.

The first mention of a house here is as a hunting lodge in 1335, described as a 'Logge of stone and timbre'. It remained a royal park until 1642, when Charles I gave it to Henry Danvers, Earl of Danby. Danvers had been in residence since 1615 and had already built a new house, surviving as the present south wing. Today the house is the result of several builds and rebuilds over the ensuing years, a tasteful collection of ideas and personal preferences resulting in an impressive and important historical home. Today it is the family home of Lord and Lady Rotherwick, who must look out and reflect on how very true the motto of Cornbury is: *DEVS NOBIS HAEC OTIA FECIT*, which translates as 'God made this pleasant place for us'.

However, we must return to the sixteenth century when the park and house would have played host to Lady Amy Robsart. On the night of 8 September 1560 Amy was staying at Cornbury at the behest of her husband Robert Dudley, Earl of Leicester, who was to meet her there in just a few short days. However, she was destined never to see her husband again for that night she fell down the principal staircase of the house. Her neck broken and she died instantly. Rumours were already rife surrounding the relationship between Dudley and Elizabeth I who, while referred to as the Virgin Queen, seems to have had a succession of lovers including most famously and controversially the Earl of Essex and Sir Walter Raleigh.

Whether there was already bad blood between Amy and her husband is unknown. However, her death was seen as suspicious and was thought to have been arranged by her husband, thus leaving him free to wed the Queen. History shows that this never happened and was probably only ever a possibility in the mind of the Earl of Leicester and those of a number of imaginative gossipmongers of the day. Such stories were further fuelled by whispers that Amy had been seen. Her ghost was said to have returned to haunt the fatal staircase and continued to do so for many years afterwards. The house was said to have continued to be her home centuries after her death.

Meanwhile the Earl of Leicester's career had continued to flourish. The year before Amy's death he had been made a privy councillor by the newly crowned Queen, itself not the wisest move considering the rumours which had started six years earlier. He had been among those who had been instrumental in attempting to place Lady Jane Grey on the throne, having a personal interest in the matter as she was his sister-in-law. When Mary was crowned she began a systematic reversal of everything she saw as wrong, she brought Catholicism back to England, executing those who stood in the way, persecuting what she saw as the conspirators' attempt to deprive her of her legal right to the throne. By the end of the short reign of Bloody Mary many of those she had perceived to be her opponents were dead, their families and colleagues discredited, and their lands and wealth taken from them. However, Robert Dudley had been pardoned and was thus able to take his place as Queen Elizabeth's confidant and courtier.

In 1587 the Queen's favourite was elevated to the rank of captain general of the Queen's armies. The next year he, probably unwisely, returned to Cornbury for the first time since the death of his wife twenty-seven years earlier. It was then he was said to have faced the woman he had arranged to meet there. Amy appeared to her husband and is purported to have informed him his life was nearing its end. He never left the estate for before he had an opportunity to arrange his departure, Robert Dudley, 1st Earl of Leicester, was dead.

Yet this does not seem to have resulted in Amy's spirit being laid to rest. Indeed, even after the house, with its infamous staircase, was demolished in 1810, she continued to be seen in and around the vicinity. Eventually an exorcism was arranged and twelve clergymen from Oxford arrived to perform the ceremony. Within months it became obvious that the exorcism was unsuccessful and Amy's ghost is still said to haunt Cornbury Park in the twenty-first century.

As parts of the estate are given over to development in order to provide necessary revenue, it seems likely the increased numbers will give greater opportunities for Amy's ghost to be seen. When properties are subjected to change it is often seen as the catalyst for the return of spectres who have been quiet or unheard of previously, thus it may be that this particularly persistent apparition may be seen more often. However, there is no reason to believe Amy's ghost is in any way malevolent. Even her appearance to the man thought central to the circumstances surrounding her suspicious death was only to give a message and not to cause harm.

It seems unlikely the ghost of Amy Robsart will pose any threat.

CHAVENAGE

CHAVENAGE HOUSE

Once the domain of Goda, sister of Edward the Confessor, the present house at Chavenage is mostly a late sixteenth-century building designed by Edward Stevens. Within the ostensibly Elizabethan façade the remains of the earlier medieval building can still be detected.

Four ghosts are said to be in residence, ranging from a lowly monk to royalty. The latter is none other than Charles I, who was first seen here just a few months after his death, famously beheaded at the hands of the executioner. To suggest the headless ghost of the former king is instantly recognisable may seem odd; however, the trappings of royalty would have been a better clue than the face of a man few would ever have seen.

Charles Stuart had come to pay his last respects to Colonel Nathaniel Stephens, an acquaintance who had fallen ill a few days earlier and had sadly succumbed to illness. It is said the king still arrives in his coach at the house, whereupon Nathaniel Stephens climbs into the coach. Anyone in the vicinity of the tree-lined avenue should keep a watchful eye out in case the coach decides to pay an unexpected visit at the same time. Within the building a shadowy figure has been noticed on many occasions, furtively sneaking around the old house. Those brave enough to approach have said it vanishes before one can get close enough to make out the individual.

CHELTENHAM

St Anne's House

This large Victorian house first saw the light of day in 1860. The first owners were the Swinhoes, a devoted couple who lived here happily until Mrs Swinhoe's sudden death. His loss hit him hard and he took to the bottle. Eventually he remarried but this was no happy marriage, his drinking and his moods made her life a misery and eventually she also turned to drink.

Entrance to St Anne's House.

Mrs Swinhoe's jewellery being denied to her increased the tension and, after numerous violent quarrels, she left her husband. After his death in July 1876 it was discovered that the jewels which had caused so much conflict had been hidden under the floorboards. Perhaps much of the trouble could have been avoided had their mother's jewellery been passed on to the children as an inheritance after her death and before their father remarried.

After being bought by an elderly couple the house was rented to a Captain Despard for his family. Soon after they moved in he changed the name of the place to Garden Reach, and very quickly the first reports of the ghost were heard. Details of every appearance were recorded in the diary of Rosina, the eldest daughter, which eventually was used as the basis for an investigation by paranormal experts. Sadly the journal was lost, although some of the investigative reports survived which refer indirectly to the original records.

Ten individuals lived in the house from 1882, yet only five of them ever saw the ghost. While neither Captain Despard nor his invalid wife ever saw the ghost, visitors and servants are known to have encountered something. Described as a tall lady dressed entirely in black, she was always reported to walk along the passageway between the bedrooms and paused before descending the stairs.

While the route the apparition took was same every time, her reaction to whatever she encountered was specific to the particular meeting. She has been seen at the writing table bent over as if penning a letter. When approaching one of the Despard sisters at the piano she was poised as if to turn the page of the sheet music. If encountering a person in the corridor she would step aside to allow passage. However, whenever anyone spoke or acknowledged her existence, she seemed surprised she had been seen, and is said to have gasped in surprise and disappeared.

The woman would appear at any time of night or day and, unlike many ghostly sightings, always appeared to be quite solid and seemed quite indistinguishable from a real person. Those who doubted the stories pointed to these as further evidence of the mistress theory. It was claimed that, with his wife being disabled, Despard had had a mistress who would have had free run of the house. It was also pointed out that the reaction of some of the household was rather matter of fact, particularly the record of Rosina, who seemed to accept the woman walking the corridors quite matter of factly, when we might expect something closer to hysteria. Indeed, it is said that everyone knew of the relationship and the ghost story was created to cover up the truth.

However, this did not explain why, in later years, reports of chills as she passed began. Furthermore, we hear of her footsteps being out of time with her movements, almost as if there was a second unseen person walking with her. Later the spectre started to open doors and also to rattle the handles of doors, whether they were open or not.

Rosina recorded that she and her siblings attempted to trap the unknown visitor. They tied trip wires across the stairs and corridors, however these attempts were unsuccessful. The woman never even attempted to step over but simply glided through them. Similarly the children made a circle around her but she passed right through between two of them. They also tried to touch the woman, but she could not be touched – she was described as always being simply out of reach. Interestingly while canines seemed aware of her, felines paid her no heed whatsoever.

Following the departure of the Despard family the appearance of the ghost began to change. Her appearance became less well defined, very soon she could never be said to resemble anything but a spirit, and eventually she became nothing but the sound of footsteps. There are reports in the early part of the twentieth century of a woman said to be a ghost walking around the gardens. However, these reports are vague at best, there is no description and it is unclear if this is the same person.

During the 1940s when the house was used as a private school there were other occurrences. No details are recorded until the place was forced to close because of what was termed 'the constant ghost problems'. During the war years when two members of staff were working late, a nun was seen crossing the playground. They took hold of a torch and went to confront the phantom. However, when the torch batteries died as they approached they took fright and ran back inside the building.

By the end of the 1950s the house – too big to be a viable proposition as a house – was turned into individual flats. One tenant reported seeing and hearing a ghost on the premises. The tenant's brother and his wife stayed there to look after the place two years later and were scared to the point that they were forced to leave the flat.

Today the house in Pittville Circus Road gives no clue of its past. Furthermore, as far as is known, there have been no sightings for over forty years. The identity of the woman is unclear. It would seem to point to the original lady of the house, Mrs Swinhoe. Had she returned again and again to find her jewellery? If so she seemed blissfully unaware that it had been removed and passed on to her children as part of their inheritance for she returned many years after it had been removed from its hiding place beneath the floorboards.

OLD SCHOOL HOUSE

It was New Year's Eve at the old girls' school. This was the year of 1939 and the war, which as everyone knew was supposed to have been over by Christmas, was not proceeding as had been hoped and the mood around the school was not good. In those days New Year was not a national holiday, but the girls had not yet returned to the school that evening, only the staff were in evidence.

As they walked along a corridor the headmaster stopped and pointed out a figure in the playground to the school nurse who was accompanying him. As they looked out through the window they saw a strangely white figure, which appeared to be wearing a habit complete with hood, approach from the far corner of the playground. The feeling that there was something unusual about the figure was compounded when the image of the nun appeared to sit on a seat which did not exist. Ordering the nurse to keep watching, the headmaster ran to investigate further. However, the image vanished almost instantly. They both noted the time, which was exactly 6:15pm.

One year and one hour later to the second the same two people were outside in the playground when they saw the same image. She approached and sat on an unseen seat. The headmaster, who had been inspecting the grounds by the light of the torch, approached with the nurse determined to solve the mystery. He shone the light of the torch beam on the image and the light promptly ceased to function. This put an end to their plans to question the figure and, with the nurse feeling very uneasy, they retired to the comparative safety of the school.

Years later the school was under new ownership, having been converted into flats. Investigations were carried out by psychic researchers to ascertain if the figure still put in an annual appearance which, by the year 2001 and if the one year and one hour was repeated, would have been expected at 7:15am on 4 January. However, the new owners felt the intrusion would alarm the new residents and permission to continue was vehemently denied, so for almost seventy years no sightings have been reported.

TOWN HALL

A building completed in 1906 and one which is the venue for a theatre which, during the Edwardian era, must have been state of the art. Not only is it the venue for entertainment but also for two visitors from the past.

One of the shadows from the past has a name and an identity. Charlie was a workman here in the last days of building. Although it is unclear exactly what his particular trade was, it is reasonable to assume his role involved him in finishing the interior, maybe plastering, fittings or decorating. This assumption is based on when the accident happened, for it was from the balcony of the almost completed interior that poor Charlie fell to his death. In later years a number of strange events were witnessed. In the theatre's boxes lights would swing with no hand or breeze to move them. Both in the auditorium and behind the scenes inexplicable chills pass through a person, while bumps and bangs can be heard when nobody is around to make them.

Perhaps these bumps are a memory of Charlie and a second ghost reputed to hail from an accident some sixty years after the first. Again there was a fateful fall, this time by a member of the public who slipped and fell down the long staircase that gave access to the theatre in the 1960s. It is impossible to say which of the unfortunate victims is responsible for the odd events witnessed when the public and many of the staff have departed. However, in these days of health and safety requirements the likelihood of a repetition is, thankfully, minimal.

GHOST OF CHELTENHAM RACECOURSE

During the years following the Second World War a couple were making their somewhat weary, but happy, return journey from Cleeve Hill. It had been a balmy late summer day and the two were taking the public footpath across the world-famous Cheltenham Racecourse on the route toward Aggs Hill.

Ahead of them on the path they noticed a man approaching from the other side of the gate which lay between them. The stranger reached the gate well before them and seemed to vanish from view. Fearing he was hiding somewhere nearby and planning to rob them they approached cautiously and upon reaching the gate, made a careful search of the area. Despite looking behind every hedge, tree and bush they could not find any trace of the man.

Some weeks later the story was told to a local clergyman. When the vicar asked for, and heard, a description of the stranger he clearly nodded in recognition. The couple were stunned to hear they had been the latest in a long line of witnesses to have seen the ghost of Cleeve Hill. The swarthy figure is said to walk the lanes and paths in and around the most prominent feature in this landscape, yet never speaks or interacts with anyone.

Hotel de la Bere

This lovely fifteenth-century Tudor manor house still stands in its original grounds. A tree-lined drive welcomes visitors who can look out over wonderfully manicured lawns to one of the most famous horseracing venues in the world, Cheltenham Racecourse. On Hallowe'en 2008 the local newspaper, the *Cheltenham Echo*, voted the hotel the most haunted place within their publication area. Indeed there have been a number of unexplained events here over the years.

Of all the reported figures said to haunt the Hotel de la Bere the longest resident dates from the days when it was a highly coveted school for girls. Said to be a former matron and nanny of the school, it is believed she was found hanging in her bedroom which is located over the present bar area. Heard pacing the room above and walking the corridors of the hotel, she is still checking that her girls are safe and behaving in a way befitting young girls of the time. Explanations of why she took her own life conflict – she could see no future for herself when it was announced the school was closing, she had been discovered embezzling school funds, she had been spurned by her lover, or she had found she was pregnant, a scandal at the time which would have made her position untenable. In truth all these reasons were probably created to fit the drama of the suicide and if any was the real reason then it is simply a lucky guess.

Over the years a number of things have been sensed by staff: a presence, a chill, a shadow, or a whisper have all led to long-term and well-respected individuals being sure that the hotel still contains echoes from its 500 year history. Some were even treated to the experience of a particular force or individual. A maintenance employee, who had worked here for over thirty years, was confronted by a 'force' which repelled, rather than pushed, him away when he was working in the loft. This was not the only record of mysterious events in the space beneath the roof, indeed one individual had the dubious privilege of actually seeing the figure said to haunt this part of the building.

As part of the continuing improvements required to keep a hotel of this size and age up to specifications and codes an electrical firm had been contracted to handle the rewiring. A big job, and one that began under the eaves where the power cables and junction boxes were located and the replacement of which caused minimum disruption to guests and staff. In the past it had housed a servant, a tea-boy who had accompanied his English master back from India in the days of the Raj and when the British Empire coloured huge areas of the world map in the familiar – for those who remember the old school atlas – pink. As the contractor was working alone in the loft space installing the new wiring, he was stunned to see the tea-boy appear before his eyes among the storage boxes. His reaction was quite extreme: he ran from the building utterly petrified and could not be calmed down by his colleagues or any of those present. The man returned to his base and reported what he had seen, vowing he would never ever return to the place. His bosses pleaded, cajoled and begged him to continue the important contract, eventually threatening him with dismissal if he refused to resume the work but nothing could convince the man to return to the job, and he was dismissed.

Such changes in a building are often seen as the reason a previously unseen or inactive ghost is disturbed. As the hotel is currently undergoing major refurbishment and will not re-open until early 2011, it will be interesting to see if the present contractors have witnessed anything and if the ghosts of the Hotel de la Bere are more active when this splendid hotel reopens.

MONTPELLIER TERRACE

One of a row of splendid Georgian terraced houses was the site of strange encounter for a rather surprised decorator. In the last quarter of the twentieth century he was in the property on his own, giving new life to the ornate rosettes so common in the plasterwork of the period.

The high ceilings required scaffolding to be erected and it was while on top of this construction that the first signs of something else being present were detected. He first felt something brushing past him. At first the lightest of touches made him wonder if it was his imagination as he was all alone in such an old property. Yet soon these sensations were very real and accompanied by whispers. There was no way of telling what was being said, although the breath of the whisperer could be discerned against the

Montpellier Terrace tenement houses, which have seen their fair share of activity.

decorator's skin. Soon afterwards paint cans left the night before in one position would be moved by the time he returned the next day and on subsequent days.

Never was there a greater incentive to finish the task.

GHOST IN A MACINTOSH

When he had first taken the job of caretaker at the college he had been warned of the ghost. At first he shrugged it off as a prank, a likely tale apparently passed on by a long line of former caretakers.

Indeed he never gave the matter a second thought when he was walking the long corridor ge spotted a man in a gaberdine style macintosh lingering at the far end. As he systematically entered each room to first turn off the lights and then lock the door, he never thought anything awry when he could no longer see him. All the warnings came back to him two days later however. As he made his nightly tour of the college, stopping to darken and secure each room as usual, he noticed the same man in the mac at the end of the corridor. Thinking this might be an intruder he approached the individual, only to be struck dumb when the figure vanished before his eyes.

On investigation it has been discovered that this same figure has been seen elsewhere in the building but never does anything to anyone.

RETURN TO MONTPELLIER TERRACE

Back to the same row of terrace dwellings and in another property more is afoot. The lady of the house reported hearing feet running up and down the staircase, she could even tell whether they were climbing or descending the steps by the sound they made. Heavy objects were heard thudding against the floorboards, while raised voices were distinctly heard coming from a room which had been empty for some time. A rapping sound had been heard in many places around the house, as had whispers, although it was impossible to make out what the whisperer was saying.

However, while the adults had only heard slightly strange things, the daughters had reported seeing some very unusual things. Once, when something was moving under the bed, they investigated to discover tiny horned lizards (chameleons?) scuttling across the floor only to disappear into the skirting board. Another time, they approached their mother from behind, only to realise as she turned around that it was a complete stranger.

CAPTAIN HARDY'S HOUSE

A man who is best known for those famous last words 'Kiss me, Hardy' – even though these were certainly not the final words of Admiral Lord Horatio Nelson. His association with Cheltenham was brief but seemingly left a lasting mark on the town and, in particular, Victoria Walk.

Vice-Admiral Sir Thomas Masterman Hardy (1769-1839) was flag captain to Nelson at the Battle of Trafalgar and commander of HMS *Victory*. Hardy rose to become First Sea Lord, as had Nelson before him, in 1830 and Vice-Admiral in 1837. During his time in Cheltenham his house there would have played host to some of the highest ranking naval officers in the land, possibly even Nelson himself.

The house has been reported as being haunted. Claims of shadows and chills, bumps and bangs have fuelled the rumours which have abounded for almost two centuries. However, there has never been any suggestion as far as surviving records show that the haunting is by Hardy himself. Indeed, if ghosts are restless spirits it is unclear why Hardy would ever be unable to find rest after his death. Unless, of course, it was *that* kiss.

SUFFOLK ARMS

An old coaching inn, where there has been a public house for over 200 years, which was the site of a tragic accident some time during the latter half of the nineteenth century. The exact circumstances surrounding the event are unclear; however, somehow one young girl was in the cellar when she was run over by the full weight of a rolling full beer barrel.

Since that time the pub has been home to the Tapping Maid, so-called because of the sounds heard in just about every room in the place but particularly the cellar. Such sounds are not the only evidence, for many have described how they have seen shadows or silhouettes in just about every room. In the cellar, the scene of the tragedy, the gas taps have been turned off suddenly and without any rational explanation.

In one corner of the bar a couple were seated early one evening when the straw in the woman's drink began to rise all on its own. We have all seen this occur when the bubbles collect around the straw and raise it up, however, this was not the case here for the drink was not effervescent.

On another occasion, when one member of the family was preparing food in the kitchen area, they left the room for a few moments only to return to find the glass of milk overturned and running all over the work surface. If that can be dismissed as a possible accident, that cannot be said of the freshly baked sausage rolls for each one of

Suffolk Arms, Cheltenham.

them had been turned over and was upside down.

All the time the maid has been reported around the pub no man has ever claimed to have glimpsed her. However, at least three females have described a young girl having her hair pinned up in a bob and wearing a black outfit under a white apron. In 2006 the landlord's mother sadly passed away, the last days of her long life being spent on the premises with her family. Her granddaughter went to see her in the bedroom and emerged to enquire of her father 'Who's that girl?' Landlord Alan assured her there was no strange girl on the premises, yet she insisted both her and her grandmother had just held a conversation with a young girl and her grandmother confirmed it.

A few months afterwards a little girl returned from the ladies toilet and informed her mother and friends she had met a friendly girl in there. The only door to the toilet had been in full view all the time and yet, when they checked, the room was empty. The girl had had no knowledge of the earlier encounter and yet gave an identical description.

When the author visited to speak to Alan, the pen he used to make notes dried up on the fourth word. This particular ballpoint had been used for some time, indeed quite recently he had been thinking it would be wise to purchase a refill in order to be prepared, so to have it run dry was no surprise. A few hours later he instinctively reached for that same pen from his breast pocket and had been writing with it for a moment or two before he remembered the pen had refused to work earlier that day. Coincidence?

EVERYMAN THEATRE

The theatre is one of Cheltenham's longest established entertainment venues. Opening in 1891 with a performance featuring the legendary Lily Langtry, since which time it has seen many of the nation's leading lights including Sir Charles Chaplin, Sir John Gielgud and Penelope Keith CBE. However, it is an anonymous individual who attracts our attention.

For years there have been stories of a death when the theatre was first constructed. When the roof of the auditorium was being completed a builder fell and was killed the instant he hit the ground many feet below. Oddly the man's name was not recorded and yet from that time he has been cited as the person responsible for a number of inexplicable events which have affected the place ever since. Known as the Dress Circle Ghost it is said that his presence means the theatre can never be fully sold out, for one seat is always occupied by his ghost.

In 1983 the place closed to undergo major refurbishment and return it to its original design. In fact it was almost three years before the place was officially re-opened by Princess Anne, the Princess Royal. During this time the workmen and staff heard peculiar noises coming from the circle, bumps and bangs throughout the building, and music coming from an empty stage. One report even mentions the sound of rattling chains echoing around the auditorium.

Since the Everyman Theatre re-opened several members of the audience have felt uneasy in the dress circle. The staff however, are unaware of any continued presence and feel that since the building has returned to its former state any possible ghost is quite content.

CHERINGTON

TROUBLE HOUSE INN

Since the time of the Domesday book there have been buildings on this site. The Waggon and Horses was the first named inn here opening in 1742. Since that time the pub has changed hands many times and even the name has altered.

This charming inn still exhibits much of the charm of yesteryear, with no sense of the tragedies that have befallen earlier landlords. Today the sign and the name reflect the suicides of two gentlemen who fell upon hard times and, finding themselves penniless, took their own lives. As the sign so graphically shows, one hanged himself and the other drowned in the river which, even today, has a nasty habit of flooding at the most inconvenient times. Hence the Trouble House Inn acquired its new name.

The Trouble House Inn signs, depicting the suicides of two gentlemen.

During the 1930s it was thought that maybe one of the former landlords had returned. Chains, once used to tether the great carts, were heard to rattle and clank without apparent cause. This was accompanied by a gust of wind which was said to run through the building. There may be a quite rational explanation for this event, for the area lies close to a natural fault line and earthquakes are not uncommon for the British Isles, indeed, there was another tremor in early 2007. Such events are often accompanied by the odd breeze so perhaps this was the reason for the rattling chains.

In the 1990s the proprietor was adamant that any number of items which he had just put down would be moved. Not by much, maybe just to the other side of the desk but most certainly not where they were left. Nobody else suffered from these ghostly pranks, so perhaps the visitor had had it in for this poor man.

However, the most chilling tale comes from the current proprietor, Martin. It was late at night in early 2007 when the building was closed and he was alone in the pub. Upstairs the family were sleeping and, as soon as he was certain all was well, he would be joining them. As with many modern premises this is one large open plan establishment and, while the doorways no longer have doors, they do still segregate the various areas of the pub. It was at one of these doorways that Martin received the fright of his life. Just as he was about to pass through the gap he felt the unmistakable feel of a hand on his shoulder. As he turned he saw a woman wearing a blue bonnet and a long dress walk alongside him and pass straight into the wall at the side of the archway. One shiver and a few goose bumps later and Martin was upstairs in the blink of an eye.

Since that time there has been no reappearance of the apparition. However, Martin has since kept his eyes open when locking up at night.

CHIPPING CAMPDEN

DOVER'S HILL

With a summit 230 metres above sea level, this picturesque setting is best known for the Cotswold Games, also known as Dover's Olympick Games. Since 1610 these unusual rural games have been held every year at what used to be known as Whitsuntide and now Spring Bank Holiday. The events are mainly on a sporting theme, including the ignoble art of shin-kicking which, despite the appearance, is a test of balance and not endurance. Hay stuffed down the trousers is allowed but only for the competitors! After the end of proceedings the whole assembly moves down the hill to Chipping Campden by a torchlight procession. The route takes them close to White Lady's Gate, an unofficial name for the region said to be haunted by a ghost also known by that name.

The author's son Jonathan, alongside the toposcope on Dover's Hill.

The story of the White Lady is a tragic one and concerns Beatrice and the years of the English Civil War. During this time a local landowner, Sir Roger, was a follower of Charles I while the family of Beatrice were staunch Parliamentarians. Such local conflict was commonplace but rarely erupted into anything remotely serious for the argument was a political one and did not affect the daily lives of the people until one side was victorious. As history records, Cromwell became Lord Protector of England and Wales and Charles I was beheaded. This resulted in Sir Roger losing all his possessions and, financially ruined, turned to robbery and became an early highwayman – earning the soubriquet The Black Knight.

One day a coach travelling to Broadway was halted by the desperate highwayman. In the coach was young Beatrice who saw through the man's mask, for she had known him all her life and recognised his voice. Before long they were head over heels in love and arranging a series of secret rendezvous at the spot which bears her name, a name which comes from their signal – the waving of a white silk cloak. Unfortunately, their liaisons were not as secret as they hoped for as Beatrice's two brothers had followed her one evening and observed the whole thing. Beatrice was sent away to stay with relatives and they kept the next meeting in her stead. On seeing the white signal Sir Roger rode out to meet his beloved, only to find himself staring death in the face at the hands of the two brothers. On hearing the news Beatrice lost her mind and was forced to spend the rest of her life in the confines of the lunatic asylum.

Chipping Campden people who have seen Beatrice, the White Lady, agree she appears on the evening immediately following the full moon, still waving her white cloak in a vain attempt to be reunited with her lover.

DOVER'S HILL AGAIN

At the top of the hill there is a car park, giving easy access to the summit. Here there is a natural amphitheatre, making it the perfect place for the Olympick Games. It has been suggested that a turf maze was once constructed here, which were the earliest versions of the mosaic patterns created in the Christian churches of the Continent. There are some examples of turf mazes remaining in England, yet they are naturally difficult to date for they have to be re-cut regularly to maintain their clear design, which means the archaeology is continually swept clean. These are nothing like the mazes with which we are familiar today, but complex pathways marked out for penitents to crawl on hands and knees around the route, stopping at pre-determined points for prayer.

Perhaps it was such a maze that continues to attract the monks seen around the summit. Several have witnessed the sight of half a dozen or so men in their traditional sombre habits. They walk from the road and slowly circle the car park before returning to the road and disappearing. All the witnesses have been standing in the field itself, looking back toward the car park, and could hear the mournful tolling of a single bell ringing out all the time the apparition was in sight.

GHOST BEAR

A traditional story retold by H.J. Massingham concerns a dancing bear, a companion of a gypsy violin player. During the earlier years of the twentieth century this inseparable duo were a popular attraction touring the fairs and fetes of Oxfordshire, Gloucestershire,

Warwickshire and Worcestershire. When in the area of Chipping Campden they would lodge, together as always, in an outhouse at the foot of Westington Hill in a region known locally as Heavenly Corner.

One winter they were seen entering the area and making for their usual lodgings, having finished another fair. The rumour went around that the man was seriously ill. Being a popular individual the people banded together and brought in a doctor to treat him, but he died a few days later. A decent burial was arranged and when the touring caravan arrived at the end of the week the great bear was handed over to them. Here the tale becomes a little hazy, some suggest the animal was uncontrollable and had to be shot while others maintain it simply pined away.

Thereafter, every winter came tales of a great beast ambling around Heavenly Corner, presumably still searching for its master. While dog owners insisted no amount of encouragement would get their animals to venture anywhere near the place when there were no leaves on the trees.

ASTON HILL

Not a particularly large area but the location where two ghosts make brief but very regular appearances. First there is the White Lady, a woman whose identity is a mystery, who is said to cross the road at the summit on the stroke of midnight. The second is another white ghost, though this time the apparition is a horse. It is also said to appear at the summit of the hill, although it is not known if this happens in the same place or even at the same time. The white steed is seen to jump over a gate at the roadside. Its leap is as majestic as any, it takes the animal high over the gate until the other side is reached and it promptly disappears.

EIGHT BELLS

A new landlord had arrived,and had only been around for a few weeks and was locking the door behind the last customer at the end of a busy night. Turning around he noticed an elderly gentleman sitting in one corner and proceeded to slide back the bolts and open the door once more, thinking he had inadvertently been left behind. However, when he turned back to escort him to the door he had vanished. A thorough search of the premises failed to find him, and the landlord presumed he must have somehow slipped out past him when he was not looking.

Next evening he mentioned the odd incident in passing to some of the long-time regulars. He was surprised to find them somewhat amused by his description of the mystery customer. The description perfectly fitted a man who had used the Eight Bells for many years until his death some five or six years earlier, furthermore he had always sat in the very corner of the bar. It seems they were well aware of his tendency to turn up to check on his old local whenever anything changed there, such as new staff or refurbishment.

COTSWOLD HOUSE HOTEL

The early 1970s is considered to be the greatest fashion disaster of the twentieth century and possibly even ever. At the hotel one lady's outlandish fashion accessories still did not stand out sufficiently for a relative of the owner to notice her presence. In fact it was only her manner which made her stand out.

When heading out to breakfast one morning the gentleman was locking the door to his room and wished a passing woman good morning. He had barely noticed her before she ignored his polite greeting and walked straight into an adjoining room. Downstairs the man spoke to the owner and commented on the ignorance of another guest. It was while describing the woman as being elderly and wearing a head of long white curls, almost as if it were a wig worn by judges. The owner was nonplussed, no such woman was in the hotel and the room she was said to have entered was certainly empty.

However, later that year this same room was occupied by a couple who stayed for a few nights. As in all good hotels, they were asked if they had enjoyed their stay when it came to checking out. While the man had slept peacefully, his wife was convinced she had seen a ghost in the room at night. She said something had awoken her and when she opened her eyes she had seen an old woman with white hair in curls, which she likened to the wig of a judge.

OLD POLICE STATION

In recent years this old building has been utilised as the home of the North Cotswold Community Radio studios. History shows that change to a building or of its occupants are often catalysts for odd behaviour witnessed by those present.

Just such was the case when the radio studios were first fitted in 2005. A series of unexplained events have been witnessed, including knocking and shuffling sounds, while whispers and hushed voices have also been detected, although there has never been anyone who can offer any insight into what the voices say. Furthermore closed doors have been known to open by themselves.

Flooding in the spring and summer of 2006 badly damaged the equipment and

The Old Police Station, Chipping Campden.

delayed broadcasting by more than a year. As a result the place was unoccupied and it is not known if the mysterious occurrences have continued.

LADY JULIANA

St James' church is, like any old building, required to have regular architectural inspections to ensure it meets strict guidelines. It was during one such inspection when four men encountered the coffin of Lady Juliana in the Gainsborough vault which apparently set in motion a series of strange and disconcerting events.

Present that day was Mr Jewson the architect, Harry the gravedigger and general odd-job man, Lord Gainsborough's agent, and the then vicar. Entering the vault, they approached the coffin of Lady Juliana, the only daughter and heiress of Sir Baptist Hicks, and Harry told the architect Jewson of the myth surrounding the coffin before them. Locals would shy away from the vault as it was said that one of the group who entered the vault would be dead within a week. The reaction of the men to this tale is not recorded, what is known is that Lord Gainsborough's agent was taken ill the following day and was dead forty-eight hours later.

The Hicks' manor house was torched by Royalist supporters to prevent it falling into the hands of the enemy when they were forced to evacuate as the Parliamentarians advanced. Locals are also said to have seen the ghost of Lady Juliana walking the length of the drive from the time of her death. Indeed, they believed the problem had been solved by the resealing of the coffin in 1881. However, the death of the agent forced a rethink.

CHIPPING NORTON

MOTHER AND BABY

As the evening darkness gathered, and the chill of the day became ever more noticeable, a young lady was cycling through Chipping Norton. It was in the years leading up to the Second World War, the 1930s, a time of concern for the future and rightly so.

Upon reaching the gates of the Chipping Norton War Memorial Hospital she stopped to allow a very young woman and her baby to cross the road. As they passed in front of her she noticed that, despite the cold which was revealing her breath in thin whisps, the baby was wearing nought but a cotton sheet and the young woman was wearing a most inappropriate summer dress and cardigan. So taken was she by this sight that she allowed her gaze to follow the woman and baby as they crossed in front of her to complete their journey across the road where they both promptly disappeared.

CHIPPING WESTCOTE

THE CONVENT

Empty for some time, the convent was in danger of becoming an eyesore. Thus the owners decided to realise the potential of the place and it was redesigned to produce homes for families.

Almost as soon as work began those living in the small community began to suspect something was awry. The atmosphere throughout the small village was unnaturally cold, irrespective of the weather. Many events, which may well have otherwise been explained as mere coincidences, were blamed on the disturbance of the convent (by the workmen) and the local vicar was called in and asked to perform an exorcism. Prior to the ceremony the reverend researched the history of the convent, a story he already knew quite well. He discovered the gardens here were previously a burial ground for the earlier occupants, the nuns.

The graves were quickly located and steps taken to avoid further disturbance. Then, over the weekend when work had stopped, the vicar performed the exorcism, since which the community has been quite content. Furthermore, when the new homes were completed and occupied, none of the inhabitants reported anything untoward.

CIRENCESTER

BLACK HORSE HOTEL

The town's oldest public house was the scene of one of the most dramatic accounts of a ghost in the Cotswolds. Much attention followed and the phenomena were investigated to their fullest extent.

The date was 13 August 1933 and, as midnight approached, Ruby Bower was sleeping soundly. The licensee's niece was staying at the inn, sleeping in a room that had recently been altered by the installation of wooden panelling, separating it from the original fifteenth-century exterior wall.

The young woman awoke at midnight and was instantly aware of something awry. Opening her eyes she found that the room was lit by a strange and eerie light. A noise attracted her attention to a corner of the room and to the ghost of an elderly and quite stocky woman with an evil look etched on her face. Her clothes were from an earlier age, the stiffness of the beige silk dress worn beneath a frilly white apron and a matching mob cap.

Ruby was justifiably shocked by what she saw. Her scream seemed to alert the woman and she hastened away through the opposite wall. It was then that she was aware of the change in the room's appearance. Gone was the new wooden panelling and in its place Ruby was aware of windows. Later her description was investigated and, behind the panelling, scratched into a pane of the glass window was the name 'James. While not instantly obvious it was certainly not there before as the name would have been memorable for it was written upside down.

The local press heard of the story and arranged a visit, complete with a medium. When the report of her visit appeared shortly afterwards the press took great pains to point out that the medium had no knowledge of prior events whatsoever, indeed she was said to be unaware even of the existence of the pub prior to this visit. Unfortunately her identity was withheld so it is not known if she was from out of town and really did have no prior knowledge.

The pub has three floors. One room on the ground floor she refused to enter, similarly she shunned the rooms on the floors immediately above it. Entering one of the bedrooms she changed, became bent, appeared to age, while her voice sounded like that of an elderly woman. Her gait was unsteady and seemed to be giving her pain. She told the others there was a great sadness in these rooms, yet when she reached the haunted room she returned to normal. Here she announced there was not one but

The Black Horse, a renowned ghostly venue in Cirencester.

two ghosts in the building. The old woman, described as having a protruding chin and hooked beak of a nose, had inflicted some pain on the man who was also said to be there. However, she took great pains to point out that the deed was done in one of the rooms she refused to enter. Ruby's room was not to be feared and neither were either the man or the woman.

The psychic told them that in order to rid the building of the presence they must follow her instructions precisely. They were to place three white flowers in the third room she had refused to enter on the third floor, at exactly three in the afternoon on the third day of the new month. All three rooms thereafter were to be kept shut for exactly three days. It seems the process was successful for there are no reports of the woman returning.

In later years other unexplained occurrences have been reported, although none appear to be related to those of August 1933.

The King's Head

Standing in the old market place, this old hotel has seen many unexplained events over the years. However, there is a link between events in the early days of the King's Head and in the modern era.

As with most ghosts, the major haunting is only ever seen at night. In the early hours of the morning, shortly after starting work as the latest individual to hold the position, the hotel night porter met a figure on the stairs. At first he thought it was a guest wandering around and asked if he could help. However, as he got closer, in the dim light he saw it was wearing monk's clothing, the cowl pulled up over a face which he could not see. The figure promptly disappeared through the wall.

In another encounter the same man was accompanied by a colleague who was interested in seeing those parts of the building rarely seen, an indication of some of the building's history. He took her to the undercroft, then used as a function room. Opening the door he did the gentlemanly thing by standing back and allowing the lady to enter first. She looked into the room and screamed, pointing at that same faceless form in the habit of a monk seated on a stool just inside the door. The monk faded from view, but the stool was still moving after the image faded. Previously this part of the building had been a monk's retreat, a passageway once led from here underneath the busy street to the cellars of the abbey opposite. The woman left her job that day and was deeply affected by her experience for some time afterwards.

On other occasions an icy hand has been felt on the shoulder, inanimate objects have moved of their own volition. The front door opens on its own, a symphonium (a music machine operated only by a pre-decimal penny) has been known to play without anyone standing anywhere near it. A guest was pinned to the bed by his arms and legs, even though there was nothing to be seen.

During redecoration some of the rooms were closed. In the middle of the night footsteps were heard pacing through this area. The doors were still locked and, on inspection, the rooms proved to be empty. Yet back downstairs moments later the same sounds of footsteps could be heard crossing through these same rooms.

Other reports may or may not point to the same individual. A pen has been launched clear across the Whitelock Suite when there was nobody there to throw it. A fireball was also witnessed in the ballroom. Observers saw it dashing haphazardly across the room before smashing into a mirror.

Perhaps these latter reports are connected with the second apparition seen here on separate occasions by a chambermaid and a porter. This second tale is one of the ghostly Cavalier who, unlike all the other ghosts of his ilk I have discovered, has not been given a nickname. Normally the Cavalier has the image of being a debonair and heroic individual, given to great chivalrous gestures and acts. This gent seems more intent on reliving the events of 1688, as depicted in a painting on show in one of the bars.

William of Orange had landed at Brixham in November of that year, starting events that would eventually see him becoming William III of England. Lord Lovelace was on his way with his men to join forces with the new king when they were attacked in Cirencester outside the King's Head. The foe was supporters of the Stuarts, oddly led by a man with the name of Captain Lorange. Although only a minor scuffle there was one fatality, a member of Lovelace's party was shot and died later from his wounds in a room of the hotel. Today that room bears the name of the victim, Bulstrode Whitelock, the same room where the pen was mysteriously flung. It is also where the Cavalier was seen firing a pistol roughly in the direction of the porter. Whilst the employee was unharmed physically, the incident had a profound affect on him and he never returned again to the King's Head.

PARISH CHURCH

Dedicated to St John the Baptist, the present building was laid out in the early twelfth century and remains the largest parish church in Gloucestershire. In a building of such an age and size it was inevitable that stories of a spooky nature should arise, the surprise being that only one exists and little is known about the woman central to the story. All that is known has been passed on by word of mouth.

It seems there was a ghost known as the Grey Lady, who emanated from somewhere along the aisle, and vanished at the point where the nave and the transept crossed. Nothing is known of her and, as far as the author could ascertain, there has never been any suggestion as to her possible identity.

US AIRMAN

Queen Anne's Column was erected in 1741, twenty-seven years after the death of the monarch, by Lord Bathurst. However, this is not a ghost of Queen Anne, although her statue may have witnessed this gentleman.

During the Second World War there were certainly a good number of American servicemen based in and around the Cirencester area, which makes identification a little difficult. However, if the next person to see him could make a note of his insignia it may help provide a clue to his identity. The American is seen leaning against the column with arms folded and looking very relaxed. When approached he is said to draw on his cigarette and speak, only to vanish before anyone can reply.

COALEY

CHURCHYARD PHANTOM

For those who have yet to be convinced or those who have experienced a ghostly manifestation, it might seem odd to find a book on the paranormal which includes stories which have been shown to have a perfectly rational explanation. However, sometimes these apparently 'rational explanations' are far harder to accept than the ghostly answer.

Details of sightings are sketchy, much having been passed on verbally, yet it seems that on at least one occasion a thin mist was seen to grow from behind the oldest of the standing headstones in the churchyard as darkness descended. The mist gathered in the vague shape of a phantom of a child of about ten or twelve years of age, before a breath of a breeze dissipated the mist in a second.

In the light of the day the area was examined and a lump of rotting wood was discovered. Investigators came to the conclusion that the mist was nothing more than the natural gases escaping from the rotting piece of wood.

A MINER'S TALE

During the days when the mines were worked a number reported unnerving experiences in and around their place of work. One individual was stopped by a ghost and, even though he did not make physical contact, felt himself being choked. Even more alarming, when his assailant spoke he used the man's own voice. Terrified, the poor miner, although he freely admitted to not being a religious man, called out to God for assistance, whereupon the ghost vanished and the man fell to the floor.

COMPTON ABDALE

PUESDOWN INN

There has been a pub on this site since the thirteenth century. However, it was when as a coaching inn during the seventeenth and eighteenth centuries that the establishment grew in stature and importance. A succession of travellers passed through these doors, including one who was suspected of preying on those who used the stagecoaches in order to relieve them of their finery and finances.

During the night the highwayman had found some of his potential victims to be made of sterner stuff and had fought back. Wounded in the exchange of shots the scourge of the highways of the day headed for the only safe haven he could, the Puesdown Inn. By the time he reached there the place was in darkness. His strength failing all he could do was crawl up to the doorway and collapse there. He was found the next morning by the landlord, having bled to death in the doorway as a result of his injuries.

Over the next 300 years there came reports of an unseen rider heard galloping along the lanes about here, conflicting with reports of a rider in dark clothing seated on a horse which make not a sound as they ride along the driveway. Of more interest are the sounds heard emanating from the room over the doorway, footsteps across the wooden floor of an empty room and scuffling sounds from the region of the old entrance. These were last reported during the 1990s after which all was quiet until 2004 when the happiest day of one young couples' life was being celebrated at the Puesdown.

As the guests entered they were to receive a glass of champagne. So one of the waitresses was positioned inside the door by the sofas with a tray of glasses containing the bubbly of the traditional wedding toast. Suddenly there was a loud crash and staff rushed around to find a stunned waitress surrounded by broken glass and spilt champagne, with the tray at her feet. She insisted she had not dropped it, nobody had been near her, and nothing had interfered with her at all – the tray had simply dropped to the floor. Being one of the more experienced staff was the reason she had been chosen to welcome the guests, yet she was so visibly shaken that she had to be replaced by another experienced girl. Within seconds staff heard the same crash, rushed around to find the identical scene of broken glass and a stunned waitress.

Quickly clearing that from the entrance a third girl was placed in the welcoming position. However, this time the owner, fearful of running out of the correct glassware, the already paid for champagne, and any willing staff, stood next to her and watched intently. Moments later she watched in amazement as the tray complete with glasses rose horizontally out of the grip of the waitress and was tipped toward the poor girl. They just had time to clear away the latest spillage and fill another set of glasses as the first guests entered. Thankfully the newcomers seemed to break the cycle and no further spillages or breakages were recorded that day, nor has there been since.

Hangman's Stone

Just under a mile northwest of the Puesdown along the A40 is an ancient crossroads. Today one road heads south to Compton Abdale and the other heads north in the general direction of Salperton. Locally the crossroads is known as the scene of a spectral horse attached to a trap. Many reports state that the ghostly transport shines as if it is surrounded by lights.

While neither horse nor trap pay any regard to the modern world, it seems one

German aircraft crew of the Second World War mistook the lights for something else and dropped his bomb load hereabouts damaging little more than a few fields.

CRANHAM

BURIED TREASURE

That evening the Black Horse public house had seen many a ghostly tale retold. As the influence of alcohol made the stories seem ever more real, Tom (as we shall call him) was taunted by his friends, for he was now living in what had become known as the ghost house.

The story had been heard many times, yet Tom felt chills on this evening as he had never felt them before. He had known the story since a boy, similar tales had been told in almost every community in the land – the miser who had buried his hoard of money, jewels, gold or silver in his garden in a spot known only to himself. Here it was a woman, who had been secretive in life and had died suddenly in middle age when seemingly in good health – or at least that was the rumour. The ghost had been reported a number of times, in the depths of night trying to retrieve her life savings.

The evening wore on and Tom left the pub before closing time and staggered a little under the influence on the short distance home. As he reached his house he saw a sight that terrified him, for in his garden was a white shape. Suddenly quite sober, he sprinted back to the Black Horse and summoned his friends for assistance, to see the horrible sight he had just witnessed.

Poor Tom was the target of many a ribbing from that day on. For even through the alcoholic haze the chaps recognised Tom's own living wife, waiting to give him a lecture for preferring to spend time in the pub instead of at home with his family!

CHAPTER 3

DEDDINGTON

MAURICE FROST

Following the end of the First World War, the quiet village of Deddington was the new home of Maurice Frost. As the new vicar took up residence at the vicarage he could never have envisaged spending the rest of his days here. Yet forty years later he died peacefully in his sleep and was buried in the churchyard.

Having no descendants it was down to his cousin to settle the last vicar's estate. Thus Mr H. Campbell Jarrett arrived from Italy and took control of proceedings whereupon the domestic staff left, not because of the man himself but because he claimed a hand had pushed him back as he attempted to leave the drawing room. Furthermore just before 9am in the morning the beds were depressed as if someone were sitting on them and yet there was nobody to be seen, while coughing was heard behind closed doors of empty rooms.

However, this was not the last we heard of the dedicated Reverend Frost. When the new vicar arrived he found his predecessor had amassed an impressive collection of books, all in excellent condition and carefully catalogued and arranged in an extensive library. Alongside the books was a remarkable collection of antique clocks, which would have fetched a tidy amount from collectors. The new vicar decided to retain every book and every timepiece exactly as they were when he first arrived in the parish.

Since that time a number of individuals have passed through the vicarage but Maurice Frost remains, returning to make sure every book is in its correct place and the clocks are keeping good time.

DURSLEY

OLD BELL HOTEL

The Old Bell Hotel is an old inn which, as the name suggests, has a long association with the Church. Yet the exorcism tools of bell, book and candle have seemingly

Old Bell Hotel at Dursley.

not been employed to rid the pub of its ghosts.

There are stories of tunnels underneath the road leading from the cellars, seemingly heading off towards the church. Perhaps this is how the phantom monk enters the building, seen a number of times around the building. There was also a report of a guest being awoken in his room by a voice calling out 'It's eight o'clock!' However, it was only three in the morning.

Yet the most active entity here has been named Mabel. Some maintain this was her real name and we shall refer to her as such, although this comes from a verbal history and is not recorded. Mabel worked as a chambermaid at the inn when it served as a stop on the coaching routes. Her main task was to ensure the beds were stripped and replaced with fresh sheets and that there was always freshly laundered bed linen available.

Her lover was a regular visitor to the inn and was present one day when a group of soldiers passed through. The military required new recruits and the life must have seemed an attractive proposition when the young men in the Old Bell had been plied with a few free drinks. Among the new volunteers was Mabel's lover, and off he went to fight for king and country. What happened to him after that day is unknown, but he is presumed to have been killed in action.

Mabel may not have been particularly heartbroken by his departure, but her mood soon changed as she discovered she was pregnant. The shame was clearly too much for her to bear, for she committed suicide by hanging herself in room six.

Since that time there have been numerous reports of unexplained activity, although none of it could ever be described as being in any way malevolent. A waitress had laid the tables in the first floor room for a reception. She left the room for a moment to collect more cutlery, serviettes and condiments and when she returned, even though she was sure nobody could have come past her through the only door, everything on the tables had been rearranged.

Movement of such items was a common occurrence. Guests would complain of visitors to their room as they slept. When questioned as to how they knew they had had a visitor they reported that their clothes, which they had unceremoniously dropped on the floor before they had retired to bed, were neatly folded when they awoke the next day. The management, perhaps quietly amused by the admission of casting one's clothing away in such a manner, would defend his staff saying they would never do such a thing – they were far too lazy and it must have Mabel, the tidiest of ghosts.

Mabel's work is not only seen in the rooms but in the bar downstairs. After a party one night the landlord had cleared the room of people yet left the drinks and glasses for the following day. Next morning every glass was neatly covered by a beer mat to keep the dust out, while those most dreadful party streamers, which can take ages to remove, were piled up in the centre of an empty table.

Mabel has not paid a visit for some time. Has she made her escape via one of the tunnels leading from the cellars beneath the hotel?

THE RIDGE

A small but busy region which has as haunted a history as anywhere in Gloucestershire. In the true spirit of the poltergeist movies this site features a new building on the site of a much larger earlier one. The earlier home had to be vacated by the resident family owing to the terrible hauntings they suffered, plagued by the appearances of a lady in white, whom they knew to be a family ancestor. Her life had ended in murder, a horrific ending which the resident family heard replayed again and again as her piercing screams filled the house.

In the land outside the house inexplicable lights were seen flashing in the trees. Horses, then the only real source of motive power, would have to be pushed past the place and would not easily tolerate returning along that way. When the house was empty during the 1920s passers-by would be said to hear the playing of a piano within the building, yet there was no piano and no pianist to play. In later decades a furtive dark figure was seen lurking near the door of the coach house, never quite being seen clearly but enough to make anyone keen to hurry their pace as they passed.

By the 1960s the place was being rebuilt, utilising as much of the previous construction as was safe to do so. The builders, already sensing a distinctly malevolent presence on the site, were horrified when a potentially fatal accident almost meant a job failed to finish. They had been gathered beneath an arch discussing a problem point when, just as they stepped away, the large heavy keystone dropped into the exact spot they had just vacated.

It is likely they finished the job professionally and in record time.

LOST IN THE SNOW

During the days when the only horsepower was the horse itself, a man was travelling to Stroud. He was to meet friends and had been journeying all day when he reached the hills above Dursley. However, he did not realise he was so close to that particular town for the short hours of daylight in the winter were already failing and darkness was descending. However, this was not his only problem for it had been snowing most of the day and he was beginning to worry as the night crept up on him.

Suddenly he noticed a light in the distance and, realising that artificial light equals civilization, he headed straight toward it. He was relieved to find the landlord awaiting his arrival. Before long his horse was safely stabled and he was in a large bedroom with a roaring fire, a change of dry clothing, and a sumptuous meal. Now warm, fed and utterly exhausted he climbed into bed and quickly fell into a deep sleep.

Next morning he awoke to find his own clothes cleaned and laid out ready to wear. Refreshed he dressed and went down to find breakfast laid out ready although nobody was around. Having eaten he searched for the landlord or a member of staff, yet could find no living soul save for his own horse. Perplexed, he prepared to continue his journey; but, before he departed he left two golden guineas on the table as payment for potentially saving his life.

Later that morning on the road to Stroud he met the very friends he had been travelling to see. Worried that he had failed to show the previous day and, considering the deterioration in the weather, they had set out to find him. They listened to his account of his good fortune but assured him he must be mistaken for there was no hostelry in the hills above Dursley. Yet he was insistent and convinced them to accompany him as he retraced his steps.

Before long he arrived back at the place where he had spent the night, yet there was no inn, no stables, no fire and no bed. What they did find was two one guinea coins in the snow.

WORKHOUSE MEMORIES

While it is perfectly natural to associate hauntings with the age of the building, there is no evidence to suggest that antiquity is a necessity. Indeed location may well be more important, as is shown by Patricia's experience.

When she and her family were the first occupants of their newly built home they quite rightly expected the place to be vacant. However, within a few weeks of settling in Patricia was awoken by someone shaking her. Initially confused, she was astonished to see a woman in Victorian clothing walking around the perimeter of the room almost as if trying to find her way out. On investigation, they discovered one neighbour had seen exactly the same thing and several in that area had heard children crying in an area where nothing could be seen. Many others had the uneasy feeling that they were being watched.

A clue to the mystery was offered when an elderly resident overheard the newcomers discussing the problem in the street one day. She told them how her house backed onto the old coal yard which once formed a part of Dursley Workhouse. In Victorian days the workhouse was the only refuge for the poor, but strict rules were observed and anyone with money was not allowed in. Thus the women, in order to keep a copper or two for the next day, would hide their last pennies in the crumbling mortar between the bricks in the coal yard. It was here the women and their children would be forced to sleep when the workhouse was full. This was bad enough in the summer, but in the winter deaths were inevitable in their weakened state, through a combination of cold and hunger.

A poignant reminder of these bleak days came when the demolition men's heavy ball brought the old workhouse down. As the walls crumbled a significant number of coins were found. Were they simply forgotten or did the owners not live through the night and were thus unable to reclaim their last penny?

CHAPTER 4

FROCESTER

BELL TROUBLES

The church just outside Frocester had seen better days. While the tower still stood firm and strong, much of the aisle had collapsed. A team of campanologists (bell-ringers) knew the peal of bells still resided in the belfry and were determined to rescue them from their inevitable fate.

One evening the team climbed the tower and examined the bells. Clearly, the cast metal bells weigh a fair amount and the largest were not going to lend themselves to man power alone. So they set their sights on the smallest bells and soon had one of them removed and somehow managed to carry it down the stairs and left it at the top of the lower staircase. A few moments later they returned to find an old lady seated on top of the bell. She was asked to move, politely at first but then more insistently, and yet she still refused to take the slightest notice of the men. Having already carried it down some rather difficult stairs they decided the only course of action was to lift it again, this time with the old lady still seated upon it. Amazingly, no matter how hard they tried, the bell would not budge as much as an inch and, furthermore, neither did the old lady who continued to ignore the men. They soon realised there was something very odd going on here, together the team should have been able to move them with ease and so they beat a hasty, and somewhat nervous, retreat.

Next morning they returned to find the bell exactly where they had left it and the lady nowhere to be seen. Obviously, they had spoken about the events of the previous evening to friends and family and one of their number had heard an interesting snippet from an elderly Frocester resident. It seems that the bell in question had been donated to the church by a female resident of Frocester, indeed she had even tossed some of her personal items of jewellery into the molten metal as the bell was being cast. Had she returned to prevent her gift from being taken from the church she loved?

CHAPTER 5

GATCOMBE

DRAKE'S HOUSE

Previously this was an inn called the Sloop. However, it is known to everyone within living memory as Drake's House. Recorded sightings of the ghost here are, at best, sketchy and with little detail – most of the information has been passed on by word of mouth.

It is said that the bearded figure appears as the setting sun drops below the horizon in the river valley. Seated in an armchair he is sitting gazing out along the course of the river, doubtless thinking of the ocean beyond and his voyages, which made him one of England's most famous historical figures. As the falling light dims from dusk to twilight the figure of Drake fades too, unsure of when he will reappear.

GLOUCESTER

NUN AND BABY

In Tewkesbury Road for many years had stood a Victorian hospital. The design was based on a house on the Gambier Parry estate, from which the place took the name of Gambier Parry Lodge.

During its history the hospital had specialised in various areas. As with many Victorian hospitals, it had been nuns who had provided care. Indeed, it was while the place was being used as a children's hospital that a terrible tragedy took place. A baby in the care of a nun had sadly died. Within days the infant's death weighed so heavily on the young nun that she too had died. However, the carer had taken her own life, and was found hanging in the living quarters of the building.

Years later this region was again utilised as the living quarters for the carers, this time providing lodging for nurses. Several reported seeing a nun carrying a baby through the corridors, a figure that appeared quite solid and otherwise normal. There were also frequent reports of a child crying, although there would not have been a child in the building.

In 1979 the building was marked for demolition, the region earmarked for modern housing. During this period workers insisted they would not work alone. They reported a feeling of sadness, a presence said to be behind and overlooking them. This feeling was particularly strong around the area of the corridor where the ghost had been seen, the morgue and the hospital chapel.

Interestingly as the building was taken apart these feelings lessened. Since all traces of the hospital have disappeared, no reports of the nun or a child have been seen or heard.

Around Gloucester

For as long as records have been kept the Bishop's House has had a reputation for being haunted by a somewhat strange manifestation, which seems to be wanting to draw attention to itself without being seen. Those who have encountered this apparition have not seen anything, not heard anything, nor have they sensed a change (invariably a drop) in temperature. Only visitors here have ever reported anything, all saying they had been assisted by an unseen hand helping them on with their coats. Perhaps the ghost is anxious for them to leave the premises as quickly as possible?

In Westgate Street number 120 was the haunt of a monk complete with cowl and habit. As with the previous ghost he seemed anxious to rid the building of anyone he could. He is said to have particularly inhabited the back rooms of the building, scaring any living thing (both human and animal) which entered. Since the place was pulled down nothing has been recorded here.

St Mary's church has an archway, above which is a room. There is a written record of the execution of Bishop Hooper who was burned alive in February 1555. The bishop was the second to hold that office in Gloucester, and he arrived in 1550 finding the local clergy in a dreadful state. He records that 168 of them could not recite the Ten Commandments, while a further 41 had no idea where the Lord's Prayer could be found in the Bible. He suffered at the hands of 'Bloody Mary', eldest daughter of Henry VIII who succeeded Edward VI and who conducted a terrible campaign against the Protestant Church.

At the prison in Gloucester has come the same repeated story for over a century. A woman is said to appear in the very same cells of the prison, where she taunts and ridicules anyone there. She is rumoured to have been a victim of a former inmate of the prison returning to seek revenge. However, this idea has probably come from within the prison itself and a more likely explanation is she herself was held in the cells of the nearby abbey. Before we question the sincerity of reports here, consider the sudden appearance of a fairly young woman in an all-male prison. One would expect she would receive a warm welcome and yet all we hear are complaints so clearly the men are more than a little concerned.

CHAPTER 6

HAILES

HAILES ABBEY

In 1242 Richard, Earl of Cornwall, was on the verge of being drowned in a terrible storm at sea. A pious man, he prayed that the Lord would deliver him safely from harm and vowed he would build a monastery should he survive to do so. As the brother of Henry III he had a few resources behind him and had duly erected the building by 1252. The Cistercian monks were obliged to site their places of worship away from society yet the land granted here made that impossible. Hence the only answer was to remove the villagers and their homes!

In 1270 Abbot John of Beaulieu visited and with him came Edmund, son of Richard, the abbey's founder. Edmund brought a precious relic, a vial containing the blood of Christ and certified as genuine by the man who later became Pope Urban IV. Such a precious item was contained within a shrine at the abbey, soon becoming a place of pilrimage to which the faithful flocked during the Middle Ages, until the Dissolution of the Monasteries ordered by Henry VIII. The Protestant Church removed the Holy Blood and took it to London where it was examined and declared to be 'Honey, clarified and coloured with saffron' by the Bishop of Rochester.

Over the years a number of stories have circulated regarding ghostly goings-on at the ruins. The monks are said to be heard chanting in the dead of night, while others maintain they can be seen wandering the area tending to the daily routine as if it was still the target for hundreds of pilgrims. However, English Heritage, who now manage the site, have never had any experiences and nobody has ever heard any reports from a visitor to the remains. There was, however, one odd occurrence about ten years ago.

An elderly couple visited the abbey ruins towards the end of the summer around the last few days of August. It was late in the afternoon, the sun was getting lower in the sky, but the light was still excellent as they snapped a few shots to remember their day in and around the Winchcombe area. A few weeks after visiting the couple had had the film developed and were flipping through the photographs when something unusual was spotted. The long shot of the area was of excellent quality. However, the region of the cloister attracted their attention for here was a shadow, a dark shape which could be nothing else but a monk wearing his habit. So convinced were they that they had caught an image of one of the ghostly monks that they copied it and sent it off to English Heritage's office here.

When they first saw the photograph the staff were perplexed, until one of their number remembered something. Around the time the photograph was taken they had produced a quiz sheet for the children, giving them something extra to keep their attention. The answers to the questions were to be found on information boards dotted around the site, the signs were stuck in plant pots and were in the form of silhouettes of monks. Closer examination of the image showed the angle of the sun had produced an image where the small monk closer to the foreground appeared to be standing in the archway leading to the cloisters. Sadly the photograph was not retained.

Hailes Abbey.

CHAPTER 7

ILMINGTON

COACH & HOUNDS

Although it should be the name of a public house, breweries please take note as it actually refers to several ghostly sightings which have become inextricably linked over the years.

The coach is as spectacular a haunting as is seen anywhere. Imagine the splendour of a high quality coach, drawn by six powerful horses, thundering along the road from Mickleton. This is the famous night coach which regularly travelled this route in the heyday of the coach, when it was the premier mode of transport in the land. It is always followed by a pack of spectral hounds, although what the connection is remains uncertain.

On the subject of hounds, there was another villager who would do anything to lead his pack of animals on the hunt. Indeed he is even said to have missed church on Sundays in order to pursue his passion, something still frowned upon even if it no longer carried the penalties of fines or even imprisonment of earlier times.

One night the man's hounds were restless and became increasingly noisy. Eventually he was forced to go out to quieten their constant howling. For some reason he was not recognised by his own dogs, who promptly tore him to pieces. Ever since the ghosts of the man and his dogs have hunted every Christmas Eve and New Year's Day. It is not clear if their pursuit is successful, or what form the quarry takes.

Another coach is seen from time to time along Pig Lane. Here is seen a headless coachman sitting atop a coach pulled by similarly headless horses. It is said to be carrying the body of a cruel and ruthless local businessman, a man who is renowned as the murderer of his fiercest rival.

The parish church of St Peter has seen the ghost of a former parish clerk make many, many appearances since his death in 1793. Edward Golding's appearances are quite irregular, as soon as it seems he has finally disappeared he makes a comeback. His early sightings were always around midnight, heard to be speaking in quiet tones as if engaged in conversation with someone unseen. Recent sightings have been during the day, near the pulpit and the altar, yet always Golding's ghost is restless and on the move.

CHAPTER 8

KINETON

BATTLE OF EDGEHILL

At the northern edge of the Cotswolds is Kineton and the site of a famous moment in time. On 23 of October in the year of 1642, one of the greatest battles in English history was fought here, the first major engagement of the English Civil War.

Had there been a decisive victory for either side in the conflict further bloodshed may have been avoided and it could thereafter have been resolved over the negotiating table. That the battle involved almost 30,000 men, resulted in 500 dead and 1,500 wounded from each side of the equally matched forces, probably accounts for it seemingly continuing long after the mortal combatants had left the arena.

Early in 1643 a report sharing the tale of Christmas 1642 in Kineton was published by a London printer. A group of shepherds, journeymen and a number of locals were abroad walking the lanes in the first hour after midnight, the first hour of the last Sunday in Advent. Suddenly they were aware of the sound of distant drums, the groans of dying men and the sounds of battle. They watched transfixed as the battle was re-enacted against the backdrop of the dark winter skies overhead, not daring to move should they be mistakenly attacked amidst the carnage all around them.

For three hours they watched the slaughter until they considered it over and that it was safe to move. They ran to Kineton's JP and minister, Mr Wood and Mr Marshall respectively, and told them of the horrors they had just witnessed. The skeptical well-educated gentlemen returned to the scene twenty-four hours later and stood open-mouthed as they witnessed the battle re-enacted once more.

Rumours spread and reached the ears of the King himself, who had been present at the battle. He sent six men, a colonel, two captains and three men of high birth to investigate and, when Saturday night came around once more, the battle was again witnessed in the skies. They watched as men they had fought with died once more, slain by a sword in the hands of an opponent.

Twice more, the ghostly battle has been reported, in the first days of 1643, and again around the early Victorian era when a group of newspaper reporters were on hand. Since that time, only sounds of the battle have been heard, although there have been reports of Charles I's nephew and right-hand man at the battle, Prince Rupert of the Rhine, being seen astride his white charger directing the Royalist Army.

KINGHAM

LANGSTON ARMS HOTEL

During the 1960s one ghost of this 200 year-old hotel started to get very busy. There does not seem to have been any catalyst for the appearances to increase to an almost weekly event, therefore perhaps the staff and patrons were simply more observant during this period.

This particular apparition appeared to be a nun wearing a headdress. The woman and her clothing were of white and somewhat hazy. Footsteps were to be heard shuffling across the floor, while strange sounds were heard, said to resemble that of muffled coughing. Room number one is the most frequently heard location for the ghost, a room where none of the dogs would enter but would stand outside with hair bristling on their backs.

The building itself only dates from the eighteenth century, although it is said that the foundations are quite ancient and an outbuilding of Bruern Abbey. As with many stories of ghosts in places associated with both a religious establishment and an alehouse, it was said to have had an underground passage linking the two. However, no evidence of such a tunnel has ever been found.

CHAPTER 9

LECKHAMPTON

LOSING CUSTOM

It was a Sunday lunchtime in 1997 and the landlord of an old coaching inn was pleased to see patrons begin to fill the bars. In the days before licensing laws changed to enable pubs to open all day, there was a window of just two hours for a lunchtime pint on Sundays. At this time the atmosphere at every local always seemed warmer and the Leckhampton Inn was no different.

The steady flow of customers kept new landlord Andy Hobbs occupied and he had no time to notice the comings and goings of individuals but responded to customers as required. Hence the appearance of an old, smartly dressed man at the bar was nothing unusual. Turning to the man he asked, 'Afternoon, what can I get you?' yet there was no reply, the man just continued to gaze in his direction while his terrier remained at his side. Turning away to speak to someone momentarily, he turned back to repeat his question, thinking the man had not heard him the first time, but the customer had vanished.

This understandably unnerved Mr Hobbs and he mentioned it in conversation with the regulars. He described the suited gentleman and his decidedly scruffy dog asking if any knew the man, who seemed to have come directly from church judging by his attire, assuming he would live locally. Nobody recognised the description and the event had been almost forgotten when a regular customer showed him a photograph of a man and his terrier. The image was uncannily like that of the vanishing customer, and the dog also had identical markings.

Sadly no record was made of the name of the gent or his pet, or of former regulars at the pub. With the Leckhampton Inn now demolished, have both he and his faithful companion found another place to drink?

LEONARD STANLEY

CHURCHYARD SHADOWS

A small village below the Cotswold escarpment which has changed little in size since its birth in Saxon times. As with so many villages in this area, sheep were the basis for the economic expansion into agriculture and weaving. Until the village became home to families of commuters in the 1960s, the place had retained its tradition of cottage industries.

In the graveyard of St Swithun's church several stories have been told of a mysterious shadow seen here. It appears to resemble a hunched figure wearing a cowl, and some have even described it as resembling a monk although none have ever seen a face. There have been suggestions that these sightings have been explained as being the shadow of a passer-by cast by the headlights of an approaching car, yet at least one person who has seen the shadow maintains there was no other person present and no headlights, just himself and his dog on the leash.

LITTLEDEAN

FIELD WALKING

During the late nineteenth and early twentieth centuries the population of Littledean became less dependent on agriculture. Today it would be described as a commuter village, home to those who choose to spend hours travelling to and from work each day in order to escape from the hustle and bustle of city life.

Since the time of the First World War witnesses have described seeing the vague blurred shapes of two women crossing a field near the bridge. They appeared to be engaged in conversation, almost as if they were out for a leisurely stroll. These reports continued until the 1970s when workmen, carrying out much needed work to repair the road surface and drainage here, made a telling discovery. At the side of the road they unearthed the skeletal remains of two individuals which later investigation revealed to be two women who must have been interred here centuries ago. Records failed to give a clue as to the identity of the women and why they were buried here, although foul play was ruled out.

A few years later locals, reminiscing about the sightings of the ghostly images over a glass of their favourite tipple in the local pub, realised the sightings of the two women strolling across the field had stopped. It was assumed that, having been reburied elsewhere, the two could finally rest in peace.

CHAPTER 10

MALMESBURY

CHRISTMAS MARKET

For those who have chosen a life on the open road, transporting goods wherever the delivery note demands, this story will make them thankful they have the luxury of a heated vehicle and a horsepower engine at their command.

Just before Christmas and Tom Crundle had taken the long journey south to the market at Bath. Here he delivered to the market stalls the homemade cakes, the freshest dairy butter and cheese and, of course, the poultry for the Christmas feast. Afterwards he toured the stalls doing his own Christmas shopping – a pouch of tobacco for his father, a bolt of cloth for his wife, the finest lace handkerchief for his mother and citrus fruit in the form of oranges for his daughter. At this time oranges were a luxury item and would have been the most expensive of them all, indeed they were probably funded, at least in part, by some of the goods on his cart being 'siphoned off' for his own benefit.

A luncheon in a local inn saw Crundle engaging in conversation with fellow carters. As they filled their bellies with a meal of beef and vegetables, washed down with a flagon of ale or two, the conversation turned to the subject of ghostly carriages which roamed the lonely lanes in the depths of winter. Of course Tom Crundle gave little credence to such fanciful notions but, as these stories were the entertainment of the day, enjoyed the talk until it was time to leave for home.

By the time Tom was close to home it was very late and the doubts of the stories of ghostly carriages must have seemed much more plausible. The night was bitterly cold, the wind driving the snow almost horizontally straight into the face of anyone unlucky enough to be perched on top of a cart in the middle of nowhere, not to mention the poor horse having to pull the load as well. Suddenly Crundle was aware he was being shadowed and saw a second cart behind him, silhouetted against the snow. Of course it is much easier to follow than to lead, thus Tom decided he would allow his companion to pass him as soon as he was able. Thus at the first opportunity Tom pulled his horse and cart into the side of the road and awaited the passing of the other cart.

Feeling much better now he was not travelling the road alone, he turned to wave a cheery greeting as the other man passed by. Yet to his surprise the other horse and cart had pulled up behind him at the side of the road. Tom called out but the man sat unmoved on his seat and did not respond. A second greeting also failed to illicit a response and so Tom forged on towards home only to find his companion was still following and taking the easy way home. Crundle objected and was determined to make sure the man took his share in the lead, so he pulled into the side of the road a second time. Once again the second horse and cart pulled in behind him and, yet again, the driver completely ignored Tom's greeting. Incensed, Tom took to yelling insults and even launched a precious orange in his direction but to no avail.

Suddenly the light improved to show that this was no cart following behind but a hearse. Tom Crundle instantly recalled the tale told just that day of the phantom hearse and how it would seek out the doomed carter and foretold of impending death. No surprise then that Tom Crundle leapt back to his seat and set off for home at a rather unsafe pace. To his horror he glanced behind to find he was once more being dogged by the horse-drawn hearse and redoubled his efforts to escape its attention. Slowly he began to pull ahead and before long recognised the lights of an inn ahead of him. The familiarity of the local gave him confidence and he hastened toward it ever faster. He reached the door well ahead of the hearse and, now feeling much more secure among friends, jumped down to await the arrival of his tormentor in order to give him a piece of his mind. As the hearse and its driver came alongside Tom reached out to grab the man and pull him from his seat. However, at the first touch Tom recoiled in horror for the man's hand was icy cold.

Tom dashed into the pub and summoned assistance. Before the hour was up the truth had been discovered. The undertaker had been attending a funeral and had travelled roughly the same route as Tom. As he made his way back in the dark he was soon hopelessly lost. In the cold he had fallen into a numbing sleep and, when his horse had found company and with no hand to steer, had naturally fallen in behind as is simply the nature of the beast.

In effect, rather than joining the next world at the hands of a phantom, Tom Crundle had helped prevent the undertaker becoming his employer's next client.

MICKLETON

THE HOOTER

A strange name for a strange ghost which produces an even stranger noise. While some stories speak of the hooter being a goblin, most consider it to be the Dun Cow.

This cow is said to haunt the wood near the village, scaring all and sundry with cries enough to make the hair on the back of the neck stand on end. It has long been told of how the animal went berserk when it escaped, threatening the lives of several villagers who attempted to recapture it. Indeed the place was not safe until the beast was killed by Guy of Warwick. Seemingly the brute is still bellowing out a challenge hoping for the chance to gain its revenge. Indeed there are three stories from the end of the nineteenth century which show just how profound an effect this had on the locals.

A young man named Hodges, together with an unnamed neighbour, had been spending the evening with a Mr Hancox. A most convivial time passed very quickly and it was approaching midnight when the two men mounted their horses and, while Hancox retired for the night, began their slow ride up the valley from Old Combe. The route was well known to them and, even in the darkness, their good spirits and the cheery conversation continued.

Suddenly they heard the awful sound and, ahead of them in the moonlight, saw the figure of an animal running along the top of a low wall. It made no sound and was said to be a calf, not a cow, which is an interesting if inexplicable deviation. Beneath them their horses were trembling with fear and it was with a great deal of difficulty and much coaxing that they managed to get them to ride up toward the figure. But, as they approached, the calf vanished and the pair continued on the short distance to their respective homes. Here Hodges asked his wife if she had heard the terrible sound but, although she was well within earshot, claimed to have heard nothing.

Years later a friend of Hodges, a Quaker, travelled a similar journey but on foot and in the opposite direction. Hodges had asked him to stay the night or to take a lantern to help light the way; however, the man dismissed the tales of the Mickleton Ghost and set off for home. Within the hour the Hodges family were retiring when they head footsteps pounding up to their front door and a loud and insistent knocking. When they let their visitor in a second time that evening, gone was the confident and hearty gentleman and in his place a pale and breathless individual who refused to speak of his experience save to say none could ever imagine what awful sounds emanated from the woodland around there.

One more who had witnessed the results of this unearthly sound was a schoolmaster. He was riding around the area when his horse bolted in terror. While the rider had not actually heard anything himself, he did think he had felt a vibration as one would with any loud and deep sound.

Interestingly there are some locals who attribute these sounds not to the Dun Cow but to two human victims from the same family but separated by many generations. The most recent tragedy occurred in the early part of the nineteenth century when the Greville brothers were out hunting in Mickleton Wood. The elder of the two brothers must have carried a heavy burden of guilt throughout his life, for on that fateful day he accidentally shot his younger brother who died from his wounds a couple of days later. Three hundred years earlier, in 1540, a daughter of the Greville family was out walking along a lane alongside the same wood. The young woman was murdered and, although her body was discovered within a few hours of her death, the motive and the murderer were never discovered.

MINCHINHAMPTON

THE RAGGED COT

A public house with a long and, at times, well documented history. One such time is the year of 1760 when the landlord was one Bill Clavers. Things were not going well for the manager of the inn: his business was going through a tortuous period to which he saw no respite.

Clavers had recently become a father for the first time. His wife and child were probably another factor in his change of temperament, for the normally placid and good-natured man had come to a decision. Aided by imbibing the contents of several tankards of ale he had deemed the only answer to his predicament was to rob the midnight stagecoach as it passed near here on its journey to London. His wife begged

The Ragged Cot.

and pleaded with him not to go and barred his way from the living quarters above the inn, standing at the top of the stairs with their newborn child in her arms. He pushed her down the stairs and shot off into the night to keep his intended villainous rendezvous.

His botched attempt was thwarted by law enforcement officers who chased him back to his home. Entering the building he discovered the bodies of his wife and child where they had fallen. As his pursuers closed in and his fate was realised, he attempted to evade a second, worse charge by hiding the bodies before they discovered he was not only a thief but also a killer. They were discussing their strategy for storming the building when they heard an awful cry of terror from within and broke in immediately. It later transpired that his scream had been caused when he had witnessed the ghosts of his wife and child cross the room and ascend the stairs at the very moment he had been attempting to hide their physical remains.

Clavers was arrested, the place searched and the bodies found. One man, as a colleague discovered the bodies, noticed a woman holding a baby watching from across the room.

HYDE FARM FRIGHTS

In the years following the end of the Second World War life was still tough. Rationing did not officially end for almost a decade and for those starting on a new life as a married couple they faced many challenges and hardships. Land that now belongs to the gliding club was then a part of the farm. It has long been associated with air travel, for earlier it had been a base of operations for the RAF. This had made it out of bounds for most, only farm workers and official personnel were allowed around there.

It was a warm day when one man broke for lunch in the field. He chose to take advantage of a small copse which afforded welcome shade after the heat in the cab of the tractor. However, he had hardly had time to take more than a bite or two when the most awful noise came from the depth of the copse. Looking up he saw a mist gathering into an unnatural form. This was enough and he fled back to the tractor and drove off as fast as the machine would allow.

Locals had always known this as a place of evil, where no birds were heard to sing and there was an unnatural darkness and inexplicable chills. Indeed many years before there had been a call for a local church to be built, thus saving the growing population from having to travel to neighbouring villages to worship. Eventually work was started, the foundations were laid down and the walls rose to half their planned height. Overnight something happened and when the workers arrived to continue the next morning they found every stone removed from the walls and lying around the site. Builders repaired the walls only to turn up and find every stone had once again been removed. After this had happened four more times work was abandoned.

No reason was ever found for this repeated act of vandalism and locals feared something evil was at work here. Since then it has always been known as the Devil's Churchyard.

RETURN TO THE RAGGED COT

When the RAF base was near here after the Second World War, some of the personnel used the Ragged Cot as their local. At a later time, when Mr and Mrs Chew kept the old pub, they found many photographs taken of the airmen mixing with the cast and crew of a film which was made here at the same time. For many years these framed photographs adorned the walls of the pub; however, they disappeared some years ago and their fate is unknown.

However, Mrs Chew was known to have told customers of disturbing events that she and her husband had found particularly unnerving. During their time at the pub their pet Alsatian, which was otherwise afraid of nothing, would never go near the stairs leading to the cellar. On a number of occasions they had heard noises coming from the empty cellar, noises which were enough to make the hairs stand up on the back of one's neck.

However, the most disturbing event was when the couple were both in the cellar and looked up to see a woman in period costume standing at the top of the flight of steps. She neither moved nor spoke but simply stood there watching them before melting from view.

MINSTER LOVELL

FRANCIS, VISCOUNT LOVELL

It is the 22 August 1485 and in a small corner of Leicestershire thirty years of disagreement is finally being decided. The houses of Lancaster and York are engaged in a bitter battle and the prize is throne of England.

Events do not go well for the Yorkists at the Battle of Bosworth Field, where the English Crown changes hands on the field of battle for the last time. Henry Tudor is victorious and, whether his claims would stand up to investigation in the centuries that follow or not, his followers are determined to hunt their enemies and quell a rebellion before it ever got off the ground.

Francis Lovell barely managed to keep ahead of his pursuers. He was heading south, to his manor house which had born the name of his family since at least the earliest years of the thirteenth century. Although this was the obvious place for him to go, and a place where he was sure to be discovered, Francis had a plan.

Francis was an obvious target for Henry's men: his father had died fighting for the Lancastrians in the same war yet he had sided with the opposition. The reasons for this change of allegiance between father and son are unclear although it seems likely Francis was simply backing what he thought was the winning side. However, following the Battle of Bosworth Field he was near the top of a long list of aristocratic figures who were declared guilty of treason. As a result his lands were taken from him and a warrant issued for his execution.

The ruins of the house visible today are of the one built in 1435, which would have been the 9th Baron's home. Prior to this the family had had another home here, erected in the twelfth century. Around 1709 the hall underwent further structural work, which was when workmen uncovered a secret chamber beneath the floor.

The underground chamber had a chair and table. When the fresh air had entered the chamber the writing materials on the table had crumbled to dust. Furthermore seated on the chair was a male skeleton, still as had it been when it had fallen forward across the table. Had the man been making notes, explaining what had happened to result in him being entombed there? Indeed was this the former Lord of the Manor, the 9th Baron Lovell who had been declared dead or had escaped the country? If so then the loss of the notes is unfortunate, for there are conflicting reports as to what happened to him.

There is some indication that Lovell resurfaced a few years later and backed the pretender to the Crown, Lambert Simnel. Whether he actively supported Simnel or not is uncertain. Other stories tell of how, having returned to his home, he locked himself in the chamber never again to emerge.

However, there is a third tale which maintains Francis gave the key to an old and trusted servant of the family. He was supplied with food and water daily in his hideaway until one fateful day the servant died suddenly. His master's fate was also sealed as, unable to free himself from his prison, the man would have starved to death.

Since that time both villagers and visitors have heard the mournful cries echoing around the ruins. Is this the ghost of Francis Lovell, his hunger pangs making him cry out in desperation? Whoever the owner of the skeleton was seems to have died a peaceful or quick death seated at his table. If only the writings had survived.

MORETON-IN-MARSH

THE BELL INN

This delightful old coaching inn has offered a warm welcome for many, many years. Indeed the author J.R.R. Tolkein, who is known to have stayed in the village on several occasions, describes an inn remarkably similar to The Bell in his works.

As a coaching inn the building was composed of two wings with a wide arch allowing access to the courtyard and stables to the rear. This is exactly as described in *The Lord of the Rings*, where the entrance is said to be on the left of the arch. Today the arch has been bricked up. However, the former entrance was exactly as Tolkein stated. Inside the layout has changed somewhat since the 1930s, principally because of the archway being closed off.

To the rear, in the area of the stables, are the beamed ceilings of the rooms. It is here where there have been reports of a rather over-friendly spirit. Several times staff and guests have reported being hugged – only briefly, not too tightly, and very warmly, but undoubtedly hugged. It is interesting to note that nobody has ever been hugged twice, even if they liked it the first time.

However, one resident, who had heard the tale several times, raised a very interesting point. It seems that the men were certain they had been hugged by someone of the fairer sex, while the women had felt the unmistakable arms of a man around them.

BLACK BEAR INN

An inn which blends in wonderfully with the other honey-coloured limestone buildings of this charming town. It is located on the west side of the main street running through the place, a road which widens to form as idyllic a town scene as can be found anywhere in the country. Driving through on market days one can almost browse the wares of the stallholders from the car. At other times the wealth of antique dealers and gift shops have something for everyone, while the choice of eating establishments and watering holes is impressive.

At the Black Bear one can enjoy a satisfying meal and a delightful pint; however, beware of Fred. He has been described as a poltergeist, yet there is nothing malevolent about Fred; he may be a prankster, but he is nothing to fear. The current licensees have experienced few of Fred's pranks. However, the previous incumbent was subjected to a number of infuriating deeds at the hands of the resident ghosts. On more than one occasion Fred was held responsible for hiding the huge bunch of keys required to open the premises, or removing the owners car keys just when he needed to be somewhere else on time. It seems venting one's anger at Fred was entirely the wrong thing to do. He responded by turning off the lights and pushing odd glasses from the shelves and causing them to smash on the stone floor.

When the present landlords arrived in 2002 they were soon apprised of Fred's behaviour. So it came about that the lady of the house, somewhat wary of Fred's reputation, spoke to him one day from the office: 'I know you're here. Please Fred, don't frighten me.' Since that time Fred has been much quieter, content to simply switch off the lights in the bar late at night when they are enjoying that last staff drink. Fred is also thought to be the cause of the phantom organ playing, always heard coming from one particular corner of the bar.

In recent times a paranormal group were allowed to spend the night on the premises to conduct their tests. They recorded the usual temperature fluctuations associated with ghostly activity and found the corner with the phantom organist to show one highly unusual characteristic. In order to record everything correctly they required accurate measurements of the room, so they utilised the laser technology measuring instruments and sent the red beams across the room. However, the corner where the organ player is said to play refused to provide a reading on the machine, it fluctuated wildly and refused to allow the readout to settle and be read and recorded.

DAME CRESWYKE

It has been suggested that Moreton-in-Marsh has more ghosts than anywhere in the Cotswolds. Furthermore the Manor House Hotel is said to be the most haunted place in the town, which makes Dame Creswyke the region's most common apparition.

The building was known as Creswyke House until just before the outbreak of the Second World War when it was opened as the present hotel. Built and re-built for successive generations of the Creswyke family it was eventually sold in 1752 to Benjamin Busby, who had founded a linen-weaving business here. Mr Busby, albeit a wealthy individual, managed to obtain the property for a greatly reduced price because one former resident was said to be still there and showed no signs of departing. Of course this was Dame Creswyke or to be accurate her ghost.

Contemporary written records are unknown, and everything documented has been reported second-hand and is at best sketchy. This is somewhat surprising considering she is said to have been murdered in the house at the close of the seventeenth century; however, there are no accounts available of the murder or any investigation, arrest or trial. Since that time there have been numerous reports of the victim being seen in and around her former home. She is said to be a busy person, the sound of her bustling gait is often the first clue of her appearance.

The dame has never been considered threatening, sinister or in any way dangerous, indeed her sole concern seems to be her beloved former home. Maybe she finds the many strange visitors to her home an inconvenience, for she is said to remove items, tidying things away and relocating pens, keys, papers, cutlery, condiments, etc. On the occasions she has been seen witnesses maintain that she seems blissfully unaware of what is happening around her in the modern era. While Dame Creswyke has been seen in and around various parts of the hotel, the focus seems to be on room number eight, although why this should be is unknown. Is this where she died? We shall probably never know what happened or, more importantly, the reasons why.

There have been other reports of a second or even a third spirit walking this building. No suggestion as to the identity of these ghosts whose actions, smashing glasses and throwing stones, make them out to be someone other than the kindly former lady of the house.

For over four centuries this lady has tended and fussed over her beloved former home, seemingly she has no intention of leaving yet.

MORETON-IN-MARSH RAF STATION

A mile outside the village is the Fire Service College, built on the site of the Second World War airfield. There are reported to be a number of odd stories told about the place, including one of a ghostly aircraft from the war years of the 1940s but investigations of these rumours proved fruitless. Indeed the only record of a reported ghost comes from the excellent *RAF Moreton-in-Marsh, A History* by John F. Hamlin and Gerry V. Tyack, and is retold here with the kind permission of the latter gentleman.

One of the oldest buildings here is that used as the 'trolley acc' room. Here the trolleys were charged up in order for them to be wheeled out and used to start visiting jet aircraft. For some time there had been problems with the electrical systems in this room – having been set to charge the power had been switched off even though nobody was around. When an Air Commodore, who had arrived in one of these jets after the war, asked if the 'trolley acc' room was still haunted it aroused interest and questions were asked.

During the war years there had been a story of a pilot who bringing a WAAF passenger back to the base had crashed into the building, resulting in the deaths of both. Very soon afterwards, when the room was rebuilt, the very real electrical problems began – it was even reported that witnesses had seen the switches moving of their own accord. Furthermore a ghostly WAAF was said to have been seen wandering around here. A second, more ghoulish, WAAF was said to haunt the control tower. Rumoured to be the victim in a tragic prank, where a Very pistol is said to have virtually decapitated the poor woman.

Where these stories originated is uncertain for there are no known witnesses of a ghostly aircraft and, as the records show, no WAAFs were ever stationed here. Furthermore, Gerry Tyack himself had probably spent more hours here than anyone, yet he had never experienced as much as a flickering light.

REDESDALE ARMS HOTEL

On the west side of the main road through Moreton is the Redesdale Arms Hotel. A well-established Cotswolds hotel with subtle combinations of the traditional and the modern, it has memories of its history in the long corridor leading to one particular room.

The earliest recorded details of any suggested haunting is in the 1970s, when room number one seemed to be the focus of attention for all the activity. Since then the cleaning staff working in this room have often heard footsteps approaching along the long corridor. Heard distinctly and getting louder as they approached room number one at the end of the long corridor, they stopped as the reached the door. Yet the door never opened and, when staff rushed to see what was happening, there was never any sign of anyone around.

In more recent times domestic staff working in the same room have noticed other inexplicable events. Each room is checked every day, irrespective of whether it is in use or not. There is an approved and predetermined layout for each of the rooms, as with any hotel, and yet even when room number one is only opened for cleaning purposes strange things have been noticed. Items had been laid out on the bed, toiletries and ornaments had been moved and placed elsewhere while it was certain that access to the room had not been possible.

Staff in the twenty-first century have found this rearranging more of an inconvenience than anything else and, as such, have nicknamed the spirit 'George'.

WHITE HART ROYAL HOTEL

Several reports have come from this building where the most famous guest known to have stayed here was Charles I. The Stewart monarch stayed here on the night of 2 July 1644, hence the change from the White Hart Inn, and a possible explanation for one of the sightings here.

As one of the oldest buildings in the village, a selection of reported apparitions should be expected. Over several decades a number of well-respected members of staff have noted doors opening and closing in the bar area without anyone passing through. It was here in the bar that a night porter, while making his nightly tour of the premises, that he saw the figure of a Cavalier. A fine sight in his period costume, complete with the hat and its impressive feather, he strode across the room and vanished into the wall beside the fireplace.

A member of staff remembers how two girls were working as maids here during the 1970s. Their adventure in the United Kingdom from their European homeland meant them staying at the hotel. Not that their stay was all fun, the room they were given was next to the laundry room. While the laundry room was never used at night, the girls' sleep was disturbed by the most awful noises emanating from next door. Eventually they were relocated and, although others stayed in the room afterwards, no further unexplained sounds were ever heard.

This was not the only place associated with the hotel where unexplained noises were heard. A nearby house was used to house staff, thus freeing up rooms for potential guests. It was a large old building where the rooms were not interconnected but reached via corridors.

On more occasions than she could remember, one senior member of staff was awoken by the sounds of stifled laughter, of footsteps and scuffling on bare wooden floorboards. Examination of any room in the place revealed nothing. She accused the younger members of staff saying they were using their access to the place for their own entertainment, although this was fervently refuted by all concerned. One night the noises were particularly persistent and, as they were keeping her awake, could not be ignored. Determined to identify the culprits she crept from the place and went to get another senior staff member from the hotel to help her search and to prevent anyone creeping out without her knowledge. Despite the sounds still being heard neither of them could find anyone else in the place. It was deemed an echo of the history of the place and thereafter those staying there tried to ignore it.

Some time later another staff member reported hearing sounds 'of a carnal nature' and the manager conducted a thorough (and to the author intrusive) investigation, which revealed nothing. Even he admitted to being baffled by the complaint of lights turning themselves on and off in a room when there was clearly nobody in the room to touch the switch.

Orchard Cottage

Two ladies were cleaning this house for the new owners. A small cottage with just two floors, it was logical that one of them started upstairs the other down. All went well until the lady upstairs heard her friend and colleague cry out. She ran down to see what was wrong and found her somewhat distraught. It seems she had heard heavy footsteps descending the staircase and had looked up, thinking her friend was on her way down, to see nobody there.

At that moment both women observed a cloud in the shafts of sunlight streaming through a window, moving in the air around the foot of the stairs. It looked like, and had the aroma of, pipe tobacco smoke. Neither woman was smoking and, as the place had been closed up for some time, they thought it a sign that the place was haunted. Indeed there have been rumours of this place being haunted for as long as anyone can recall, yet this is the only known occurrence.

St David's

During the twentieth century a recurring tale of an apparition has surfaced around the churchyard here. While each time the story is different, there are distinct similarities in the tales and they are probably different viewpoints of the same story. As with many churches of this age it stands on a mound, making the graves higher than the road. Over the years there have been a number of reports of a ghostly male emerging from the wall surrounding the churchyard and crossing the road towards what was the school and neighbouring buildings.

Nobody has ever suggested which grave the figure comes from, nor is there any confirmed report of any activity in the buildings opposite.

Lemington House

If anyone is to perceive an apparition and not be concerned, an olfactory one seems to be the best method. Such has been reported by a number of people at this house in Moreton.

For the last twenty years a strange and unexpected aroma of orange blossom has been detected. There is no orange blossom anywhere nearby and it does not always coincide with that particular part of the growing season. For those who have never experienced the scent it is to be recommended for, as one resident here remarked, the sense of tranquillity that accompanies it is most welcome. Here that feeling comes as soon as the aroma is detected and, strangely enough, is also as clearly missed when it disappears moments later. Experts agree there are no other aromas which could come from the building or its surroundings which could be mistaken for that particular scent. Thus it remains a mystery.

Perhaps this smell is a secondary warning that in an upstairs window an old face has been seen looking out, even though the place is known to be empty.

Fosse Way

This old Roman road, today designated the A429, takes its name from the drainage ditch which set it apart from existing trackways before the arrival of the great empire almost two millennia ago.

It is the railway bridge which interests us here, for this is the focus for a number of unexplained reports. Most concern odd noises said to emanate from a number of places including a building belonging to the old gasworks and a number of different houses. The description of 'odd' noises refers to them being unidentifiable which, when combined with the number of places, does not help to understand the cause.

However, the oddest reports concern a motorcyclist. One local spoke of seeing a man on the machine crossing the bridge. He was not wearing a crash helmet but the age of the vehicle would suggest this was not a legal requirement when these were on the road. However, another insisted not only his helmet was missing but also his head. These tales are not unlike those heard from three men travelling in a car across the bridge in August 1997, shortly after nine in the evening. As the aging vehicle closed in behind their car it suddenly vanished.

Pond Troubles

November 1916 was not the most pleasant of times, as there was no end in sight to the Great War and the coming winter must have added further gloom for the locals. Near the Horse Pool was a public house which afforded some comfort and, it seems, rather too much for one man who staggered out late that night in 1916. The following morning his body was found in the pool, he had somehow got himself lost and had ended up in the deepest part of the pond where he had drowned.

The houses around here are said to have encountered a number of odd events over the years. One was when the doors were knocked by an unseen figure, another speaks of footsteps pacing back and forth along the upstairs landing but nobody was there, while others have said to have felt people brushing past them and even hands momentarily tugging at their person. One lady, walking past the pond around thirty years ago, saw a tramp soaking his feet in the pond. His leering grin troubled her and she hurried past, yet when, mere seconds later, when she turned around to make sure she was putting some distance between them, she saw he had vanished without a trace.

MORETON HOSPITAL

The locals who have been associated with the hospital all agree the identity of the ghost is none other than the first matron in 1873, Miss Rebecca Horne. She had a reputation for being a demanding but fair individual, a stern countenance but a kind heart, and a woman who set exacting standards, really the quintessential matron so often depicted in old films. Whilst it would be difficult to recognise a woman in uniform from others, especially when her face was known by very few, she is known to have kept cats, always white cats, which tended to identify her.

One sister on night duty saw a nurse hurrying along a corridor and, thinking an alarm had been raised, hurried after her to offer assistance. All thoughts of a troubled patient evaporated when she witnessed the nurse vanishing through the wall at the end of the corridor. This is just one of many examples of unexplained events and always on the night shift. Nurses have heard locked doors opening and closing, footsteps echoing along empty corridors, patient alarms sounding when the patients have not activated them, and a figure in a nurse's uniform flitting around the building at all hours.

Upstairs an impromptu bed had been thrown together to allow nurses to grab a couple of hours rest when on the long stretch of night duty. Several nurses have felt the unmistakable sensation of a cat walking across the bedclothes and settling down next to them. However, when they turned on the light there was no animal to be seen. All this activity seems to come in bursts, periods of high activity interspersed by long years of nothing.

It seems the hospital is well overdue another visit from Miss Horne.

CHAPTER 11

NAILSWORTH

A SEATED GHOST

The countryside around Nailsworth is well worth taking the time to enjoy. Aside from the tarmac surface, the tree-lined roads around here have changed little for many years.

One gentleman has been seen sitting quietly on a bench enjoying the scenery. He seems oblivious to anything or anyone around him, paying no attention to passing traffic whatsoever. He has been seen for many years, yet any attempt to identify him or which era he belongs to is made extremely difficult. His attire appears to be that of a farm labourer, which could come from just about any period.

More intriguing is the bench upon which he sits. Some maintain it is also a part of the apparition and cannot be seen without him. Having made a thorough search of these lanes I found no bench, ghostly or otherwise.

NAUNTON

OPEN ROAD

The principal road serving Naunton is the B4068, which follows the contour lines to the south of the village. It is along the road itself, rather than the village, which is the focus of attention. All the reports are quite recent, the earliest being from 1998 when a woman in white with contrasting black hair waved to a passing motorist. Slowing to see if she required assistance, he was amazed to see her vanish in front of his eyes. The driver, a doctor, brought his vehicle to a stop and looked around to see if she had disappeared among the hedgerows, thinking maybe his medical training would be of some value, but there was nothing and no one to be found. It was during the summer and the light that evening was still good, indeed the doctor was able to see the woman in question was wearing a sleeveless dress.

Two years later the new millennium arrived and the white glow of a ghostly monk was seen along the same road. However, this man did not seem to be aware of the vehicle coming up behind him and allowed the vehicle to pass right through him as the driver braked sharply.

Yet surely the strangest tale tells of how a vehicle travelling along here suddenly lost power. Nothing unusual about that, mechanical devices are not perfect and will fail to work occasionally. Even the return of the drive from the engine moments later is quite easy to explain. However, the period in between coincided with those travelling in the vehicle reporting a feeling of water running over their feet, although they neither saw any water nor were their feet or shoes wet afterwards.

NETHER LYPIATT

IRON GATES

Since 1981 the manor house here has been home to Prince and Princess Michael of Kent. This house in Gloucestershire had always caught their eye and they were keen to purchase when it came on the market. Originally the asking price was considered too high but tales of its ghosts put off many prospective buyers, and eventually the price was reduced to an affordable £300,000.

Prior to the royals moving in here it had been the home of Violet Gordon-Woodhouse, a renowned exponent on both the harpsichord and the clavichord. She was the sister of a Member of Parliament for Eastbourne, while another brother became the mayor of that town. She was rumoured to have shared a bed with John Bodkin Adams for many years, a doctor who was suspected of causing the deaths of 160 people under his care although the cases against him were never proven.

Earlier, Violet and her home were the talk of the society gossip pages as the nineteenth century turned to the twentieth. She married Gordon Woodhouse in 1895, accepting his proposal only on the understanding they would always have separate bedrooms. Her string of lovers was unlikely to have been as long as was rumoured. However, she made no attempt to cover her promiscuity, almost flaunting it, and revelling in the publicity.

In 1899 she moved one of her lovers, Bill Barrington, in with them. Max Labouchere was another lover who joined them in 1903, while by the time Dennis Tollemache arrived two years later her husband must have been wondering if this would ever end. However, it seems a husband and three lovers was enough for Violet.

The house was built at the beginning of the eighteenth century by the renowned local judge John Coxe, who was renowned for the severity of his sentences and employed the hangman's noose whenever he could. The circumstances behind the tragedy involving Judge Coxe's son have never been made clear. All we really know is he was found having hanged himself in one of the upstairs rooms. This is the individual who is said to haunt the house, most often seen walking the magnificent staircase that runs throughout the house.

Standing in eight hectares of gardens, the house originally formed a perfect square measuring fourteen metres on each side. Within its four floors, which include a basement and attic, are four bathrooms, four reception rooms, eight bedrooms, two dressing rooms and staff quarters. Wooden panelling and a staircase made from an imaginative use of chestnut, oak and beech make this a very desirable residence indeed.

Approaching the building the first thing to be seen are the quite splendid pair of gates. The year was 1704 and the judge was presiding over a case involving the local blacksmith. Just what his crime was is uncertain, some accuse him of murder, others of stealing a sheep. Both crimes carried the death penalty and Coxe lived up to his reputation by sentencing the blacksmith to the gallows.

However, the judge was never one to pass up a chance and offered the metalworker the chance of a reprieve. If he could produce a pair of perfectly matching gates to the requested design without a single blemish, and without asking a penny for the work, the guilty man would be allowed to go free.

Obviously this was a way out for the blacksmith which he was not likely to pass up. For two weeks the man toiled his every waking hour and produced the wondrous gates which adorn the manor house today. However, the judge scrutinised the gates so closely he found the tiniest flaw, which was doubtless always his plan. Thus, now the judge was in possession of a quite wonderful pair of gates which had cost him nothing, the reprieve was denied and on 25 January 1704 the blacksmith was hanged.

However, this was not the end of the story, for every year on the anniversary of his death as soon as the hour of midnight is reached the gates fly wide open on their own. Through the yawning gap rides the large figure of the blacksmith astride a galloping white horse.

NORTH NIBLEY

A PRIVATE LITTLE WAR

It was 20 March 1471 and to the northwest of the village at Nibley Green two rivals are battling for supremacy. This is a significant day in English history for the battle between the forces of Lord Berkeley and Lord Lisle was the last time private armies ever fought on English soil. Reports have come through of the sounds of a ghostly battle being fought, people having heard the sound of horses hooves, the clashing of swords, the whoosh of arrows in flight, and the moans and shrieks of the wounded and dying on the field of battle.

Lord Berkeley's men were known to have camped on Michaelwood Chase the previous day. Here on 19 March each year the marching men and horses can still be heard on the anniversary of the eve of battle.

HORSE AND RIDER

Driving her car down the lane through Nibley Green, a local woman was amazed to see a horse and rider suddenly vault the hedge on her left side of the lane. She noticed how both the animal and its rider seemed to shine with an unearthly glow. The car was not travelling particularly quickly and she brought it to a stop level with where the horse had appeared. By this time the horse had leapt the gate on the other side and entered the field.

Although it was only a few seconds after the horse had entered the field, when she looked over the gate neither horse nor rider could be seen and yet there was not a single obstruction in the field to hide them from view. Somewhat unnerved, she quickly returned to her vehicle and left the scene.

GHOSTLY FUNERAL

On the eastern boundary of the village, in the direction of Waterley Bottom, are two bridges. Between these two is an old lane which was long said to be where a phantom funeral procession can be seen. The line features a horse-drawn hearse and a number of mourners, all of whom have their heads bowed and thus are hiding their faces. As the driver of the hearse nears the observer he lifts his head to reveal his identity. It may be anyone known to whomever is watching, even a reflection of their own face. However, it is said that whoever is seen as the driver of the hearse they will be dead within a year.

The hearse is only seen on a single night each year, thus if that date is known then it is a simple matter to evade that area on that night. However, some years ago the overhanging trees, which made this a very dark and gloomy lane, were cut down and since that day the procession has never been seen. Indeed it has been so long since anyone saw the procession that not a living soul can recall the date on which the phantom hearse travels the lane.

NYMPSFIELD

BRONZE AGE BARROW

When archaeology was still in its infancy this 3,000 to 4,000 year old site was being excavated by Captain H.S. Gracie. Within the tomb had been found human bones, not neat burials but a jumbled collection of bones. As was the practice at the time these bones had been placed inside the tomb after the flesh had been removed – either deliberately or naturally.

The chamber containing the bones had been uncovered and was open to the elements. Captain Gracie was walking there with his dog one day when his pet climbed the mound and deliberately dropped into the hole beside the bones. Acting completely out of character, it stood rigid with fear at first, then howled and ran off without waiting for its master. The archaeologist, more concerned for the historical relics, was convinced he would find the dog waiting for him at home later that day and thought no more about it. He turned his attention to extracting and carefully wrapping the bones to be sent away for analysis. It was later revealed these belonged to no less than twenty-eight quite separate individuals.

It came as something of a surprise to find the dog missing when he arrived home, indeed it was two days before he laid eyes on his pet again. Within a day or two of returning home he accompanied his master back to the ancient burial site and, as before, leapt into the excavated chamber. However, this time the bones had been removed and the dog was completely unperturbed.

Bronze Age barrow at Nymspfield.

CHAPTER 12

OWLPEN

Described as 'The loveliest place in England' by *Fodor's Britain Guide* in 2002 and 'The epitome of the English village' by no less than HRH The Prince of Wales in *A Vision of Britain*, I was beginning to wonder if my interest in the place would be appreciated. I had not considered that this village situated east of Uley might actually be quite proud of the number of ghostly happenings reported here.

My first encounter with Owlpen was on a walking holiday in June 1987. In what had to date been a rather damp summer, the heat of that Saturday was particularly sapping on my legs and so I took a few moments to view the interior of Holy Cross church. Entering the church I found the visitors' book and my eyes were immediately drawn to the last entry in the book, someone from Australia by the name of Poulton had visited the previous day.

My other memories are of a quite magnificent beech tree and Owlpen Manor, which positively glowed under the bright sun. At that time, over twenty years ago, I had no idea of the ghost stories which I would later be putting into print, if I had I may well have taken a much longer rest and a much shorter walk that day.

With no less than four quite distinct figures having been reported here, it is to the best known that we first turn our attentions.

THE QUEEN'S CHAMBER

The queen in question is Margaret of Anjou, consort of Henry VI, who stayed in this room on the night of 2 May 1471 with the room being named in honour of her visit. She was travelling to offer her support to the Lancastrian troops led by the Duke of Somerset at what history would later record as the Battle of Tewkesbury, fought on 4 May 1471.

History shows the Lancastrian defeat as one of the pivotal battles in the Wars of the Roses. Yet worse news was to follow. Her son, Prince Edward, the only surviving legitimate heir of Henry IV, was brutally murdered here. Queen Margaret fled, but was captured and imprisoned for four years until ransomed by Louis of France. The Lancastrian defeat at Tewkesbury left their forces despondent and the country remained mostly peaceful for the next twelve years.

Over the previous decade the Queen had earned a reputation for being ruthless and aggressive, yet the loss of her only son changed her. On her return to Anjou in France she became a recluse and died in poverty in August 1482. It is often said that she claimed her last happy night was the one she spent at Owlpen, so it should not be seen as too much of a surprise if she has returned.

Many have described the grey lady with her fur-trimmed gown, tall hat and the fifteenth-century head and neck covering worn by women and known as a wimple. It was not only those who knew roughly what she would have worn who gave this description. During the Second World War children from Birmingham were evacuated to Owlpen, they would have no idea what or who she was, and yet they described her in great detail.

THE MONK'S BONES

The Manor's east wing is said to be home to a monk. This hooded figure has been seen moving furtively around this part of the building and has become known locally as the Black Monk, amongst other things.

A number of conflicting suggestions have been offered as to the identity of this individual. One says he was a member of the resident de Olepenne family, who lived here throughout the Middle Ages and who clearly take their name from the place. A document tells of the death of one member of the family, a Benedictine monk at St Peter's Abbey in the city of Gloucester.

A second and somewhat more chilling narrative concerns the monk who fled Kingswood Abbey near Wotton under Edge at the time of the Reformation. He ran the eight kilometres across country to Owlpen where somehow he was walled up. It is assumed he had help, as surely if he had bricked himself in he would have left himself a means of escape. Instead the man starved to death.

Years later it was discovered that the dimensions of that room were too small, revealing there was a space behind. When the false wall was taken down the monk's bones are said to have crumbled as soon as the light hit them.

CHAPTER 13

POULTON

ELIZABETH BASTRE

This tale may well be unique, as more is known about the apparition since her death than was ever known about her life. Stories concerning her life are both confused and conflicting, with an array of reasons being given. However, one thing seems certain, for reasons which have never been adequately recorded, Elizabeth Bastre was not buried in consecrated ground. The two most often quoted reasons for this are that she was a witch or a suicide, and one story cites her as both!

Take Bell Lane out of the village of Poulton and, heading north, we meet the road running northeast from Ampney St Peter to Quenington. Examine the Ordnance Survey map and shortly before the junction on the right-hand side of the lane is the marked site of Betty's Grave. Furthermore, we know she died and was buried here in 1786. This, the last resting place of a named individual appearing on an official map, may well be unique.

However, was she a witch who took poison to evade justice? Or was she hanged, either for witchcraft or sheep rustling? Either way her grave was deliberately placed here, at the place where the two roads already mentioned combined with that heading north towards Arlington to make the classic crossroad burial. It is said the spirit of the miscreant will search for the correct route to salvation and, unable to choose which, is thus trapped. Yet there are two other versions of her death, one relating how she had died from exposure after challenging a farmer to perform a task (at least four different tasks are cited) faster than she, while another suggests she was a murder victim, a servant killed by her master.

Whatever the reason for her body being placed here it seems to have worked for she is still said to wander about the area, still seeking the route to eternal peace.

PRESTBURY

DEEP STREET

Historically the lands of Prestbury have been held by two powerful and greatly influential churches. Both Llanthony Priory, that provided the parish with a priest, and Hereford Cathedral, that established a hunting lodge, made good use of the village.

While the Bishop of Hereford spent vast sums of money on lavishly entertaining guests, the monks left a more permanent reminder of their holdings. In Deep Street is found Reform Cottage, a sixteenth-century building which stands well back from the row formed by the other buildings in the street. While there has never been any evidence to support the claim, it is said that the ground between the road and the cottage was used by Llanthony Priory as a burial ground for their monks. Perhaps it is one of these who still walks the grounds.

The ghost of Deep Street seems to have a good knowledge of the modern calendar, for of the three occasions he emerges each year one, that of Easter, is a movable feast. He is also said to emerge on Christmas Day and All Saints' Day, and always after dark. The first indication comes when footsteps are heard approaching the cottage, yet, there is no knock on the door. Moments later footsteps are heard upstairs crossing the attic, accompanied by crashes and bangs as if the place is being turned upside down. However, when the attic is examined no sign of any entry is evident.

As with many ghost stories associated with buildings alongside or near to the church, it has long been held that a secret passageway runs between Reform Cottage and the local place of worship. If it ever existed no record of it has ever been found, nor has anyone ever suggested a reason for its existence.

THE GALLOPING GHOST

Correctly that should be 'ghosts', for there are two quite distinctly unexplained phenomena. One features a knight in full armour but lacking heraldic symbolism which might help to identify him. Clearly this gentleman still observes the rules of chivalry, for he always pauses during his ride to gesture a salute before galloping off into the distance. This is not the case with our second phantom horseman, whose ride seems to end very abruptly indeed. Prestbury's second rider has been reported along several lanes, although he is said to be the spirit of a Cavalier who was captured during the English Civil War by the Parliamentarian supporters who were resident in Prestbury House. They were in the habit of putting up a roadblock, albeit a rather makeshift one in the form of a rope strung across the road outside their home.

One evening they succeeded in unseating one of the king's despatch riders as he rode at full speed through the village. Knocked senseless by the fall he was easily captured and executed there and then. Still he is heard charging through the quiet lanes of Prestbury, the galloping hooves heard approaching only to cease abruptly.

However, this second horseman has also been said to have been heard to come to a more normal stop, the rider dismounting and entering the house. It was here some thirty or so years ago that two workmen were chased from the building by a very old man with a long white beard who was armed with a stick. He brandished the walking stick in their direction and forced them to leave before they had a chance to even begin working.

CLEEVE CORNER

Of all the ghosts here, Prestbury has only one which could be said to be vicious. In a bedroom of a seventeenth-century farmhouse close to the church a murder took place.

Here a young bride was resting shortly after her wedding. She had with her a collection of wedding gifts and some of the family jewellery presented to her by her father, effectively her dowry. Obviously a wedding is a very public affair and there is the potential for a thief to see an opportunity in the form of the gifts and valuables which are traditionally given to the newlyweds. The identity of the woman who was found strangled here is unknown. However, she had apparently been the victim of a theft. It was suggested that she had been killed by her husband for her dowry, but this does not seem a likely motive as he was already effectively the recipient of everything.

Since that time those who have slept here are warned they might be woken in the night by an evil presence in the room. A strange light and the cold and clammy atmosphere are most unsettling. Some have reported a pressure against the throat as if being strangled. As the grip tightens a prayer will save them from becoming another possible victim in this room.

OLD MOSES

This may well be the Cotswolds most whimsical spectre. Prestbury is virtually on the doorstep of Cheltenham racecourse, and was home to Fred Archer, one of this country's most famous jockeys. Fred has been said to have returned to haunt but at Newmarket, not at Prestbury and the old coach house known as Walnut Cottage.

The cottage is the haunt of Old Moses, who seems particularly fond of appearing in the dining room, as he himself once put it 'just to see how things are'. One owner, perhaps while trying to convince himself that his home was not haunted, sat at the table for dinner and stated loudly he did not and never would believe in ghosts and the mirror promptly fell off the wall.

There is some disagreement as to who Old Moses was. Some stories tell of the racehorse trainer who would get his own way by any means possible. However, the degree of his misdemeanours vary considerably, and are somewhat vague, which probably tells us these stories have been created to fit the character. Old Moses was probably the groom who lived at the cottage for many years during the nineteenth century.

The last record of Old Moses was in 1961; however, do not discount his return for such gaps between his appearances are by no means unheard of.

Sundial Cottage

A place with an apparition which seems to have a musical bent. However, the identity of the individual is unclear.

Anyone passing this charming old cottage, especially on those warm summer evenings, should keep an ear out for the playing of a spinet, a compact upright piano. No mention has ever been made of the melody, or indeed if the same tune is heard each time. However, the player is another matter.

Towards the end of the nineteenth century a professor of music gave private lessons in the one room of the cottage. Some believe this to be the identity of the ghost, still playing in the same room in which he gave the lessons. Others point to a pupil of his, a young girl, who has been seen walking around the garden wearing a summer dress.

High Street

Nothing pleases a ghost hunter more than a ghost whose appearances form a pattern, for this makes further sightings potentially predictable. Prestbury has one such apparition, although the dates are a little uncertain for Christmas and Easter are quite lengthy periods of time and the latter is a movable feast. It seems likely the ghost here is a religious figure, for not only do his appearances coincide with the two most important Christian festivals but he is first seen materialising in the church itself. From here he crosses the churchyard and walks along high street before disappearing through a wall. Investigations have failed to reveal any logical destination for the gentleman.

There were reports of a photograph of the event being taken around twenty years ago. Yet nobody was aware of either the photograph or the supposed photographer.

OTHER PRESTBURY GHOSTS

One old lady seems to enjoy a stroll along Main Street at night. She is dressed in clothing associated with medieval times, or possibly earlier, and pauses to look in through the windows of the buildings almost as if she is window shopping. As she reaches the Almshouses she promptly disappears.

Animals are not as often seen in ghost stories as people. This is simply because our furred and feathered friends have no clothing to show them to be from an earlier time, nor are they particularly recognised as being specific individuals. Thus they are most often recognised by the company they keep. Such is the case with the shepherd seen, complete with ghostly flock, in Swindon Lane, Prestbury on a foggy autumnal night in the 1970s.

It has been said the reason for drovers, horse riders and dog walkers avoiding the route along Mill Street and Mill Lane, if at all possible, is due to another ghostly figure. This presence appears, along with a feeling of cold, as a white misty form gliding in and around these lanes and the neighbouring fields. It is known as Mrs Preece's Ghost, although who she was and the circumstances of her death are unknown.

CHAPTER 14

SALPERTON

ALL SAINTS' CHURCH

To any Englishman old enough to remember that glorious occasion at the national stadium in the summer the year of 1966 was an unforgettable one. For very different reasons a group of individuals gathered at the mansion house in Salperton also had good reason to remember that year. They watched as an attractive young woman wandered around the neighbouring churchyard. If their attention was drawn by such an unusual sight, their mood turned to one of shocked disbelief when they saw her walk up to a tomb and vanish.

Quite clearly such a mysterious occurrence required further investigation. Enquiries revealed that the tomb in question was that of a woman of nineteen or twenty years of age. Furthermore, inside the church is the most gruesome reminder of a terrible murder some years before. Locate the pulpit and on the stone floor around it is the dark mark of an age-old bloodstain, the last remnants of the victim, which have remained despite all attempts to clean it off.

SHIPTON OLIFFE

FROGMILL INN

Parts of this pub are over 1,000 years old, thus it would be more surprising if there were no stories of unexplained and mysterious events. As it turns out there have been at least three strange events reported here, none of which would seem to have a rational explanation.

Although there were reports dating from earlier, the first time anyone bothered to put anything in writing was shortly after the end of the Second World War when, over a period of twenty years, there seems to have been almost as many hauntings as paying customers.

One fairly regularly reported occurrence was the mist. It invaded the building creeping around and touching uncovered flesh with a coldness which could never be adequately explained. The mist would be surely expected, for this place still has a waterwheel, a remnant of the watermill, at one end of the property, and there is more than enough water around here to create a mist. However, the mist was seen in thin wisps creeping through the building well away from the waterwheel and the water, indeed that part of the building nearest the water was quite clear as was the outside. This phenomenon has not been seen for over forty years and therefore has not been subjected to modern testing procedures and recordings which may provide a rational explanation for the strange mist. Sometimes the witnesses have reported not only mist but whispers too. No pattern has developed and nobody has ever been able to hear what message the whisperers were trying to convey. Incidentally, some of the witnesses suggest the whispers are coming from the ceiling and that more than one voice can distinctly be heard.

Yet the most unusual report came from a guest. It was early evening and the light was still good. The curtains had been closed for privacy and the guests were getting ready for the evening meal and a glass or three of their favourite tipple. Illumination was being provided by electric lights and the television was on in the corner of the room, with the sound turned down low awaiting the evening news programme. Suddenly three figures appeared at the table in the room, they were playing cards and seated around a table in the room but apparently not playing on it. Indeed it was almost as if they were playing on a ghostly table. The image was brief, lasting only a few seconds before vanishing and, as far as we are aware, has never returned.

Change is usually the catalyst for any appearance and, at the time of writing, the premises are on the point of changing hands again. It remains to be seen if the apparitions will return.

SNOWSHILL

CHARLES MARSHALL

During the nineteenth century Charles Marshall was resident at Snowshill Manor, as pleasant a stately home as can be found anywhere in the Cotswolds, dating from the late fifteenth century. For over fifty years it has been a National Trust property and, during this time, has been blamed as the ghostly visitor often seen in various rooms by the staff.

With the house went over 400 acres of farmland which, after Mr Marshall's death, passed to his widow. She continued to run the estate just as her husband had done previously, until a few short years before her death in 1858. It was then that the house underwent a good deal of work to repair and extend the building, work that would have cost an appreciable sum of money. How the widow Marshall financed such extravagance may have been revealed in 1919 by Richard Dark who had married the daughter of Richard Carter and was formerly a trusted farm worker and a particular favourite of the Marshalls.

It was a cold day in winter and twilight was falling. Richard Carter, who had been working at Hill Barn, made his way home along a little-used lane through the estate. One evening he was approached by a figure riding a black horse. He was astonished to find the man in the saddle was none other than his former master, Charles Marshall. This happened several times, each time the ghost rode alongside him Carter rode off as fast as he could.

Eventually Carter resorted to consulting the local minister. He was advised that it was likely the figure desired something of him and he was to challenge him next time, demanding to know why he would not leave him alone. Thus the next time he was approached he confronted the ghostly figure exactly in the manner he was told. The ghost responded by telling Carter to meet him again that night at midnight in the chaff house, a farm building used to store fodder. The labourer, overcoming his fears as he wanted to end the meetings, turned up at the appointed hour and was given a message for Mrs Marshall.

Seemingly only the messenger and the Marshalls ever knew the contents of that message. Yet it is assumed that, with the building work north of the manor house which ensued soon afterwards, it was a message revealing where Charles Marshall kept a secret hoard of money.

From that time no further sightings have been recorded of Charles Marshall.

Ann's Room

A number of the rooms at Snowshill Manor are named to reflect the history of that room. There is a Zenith room, supposedly where a duel took place, one of the combatants having died there and hence the name. Other rooms are dedicated to the strange collections of former owner Charles Wade, an eccentric but likeable man who was particularly keen on mementoes of witchcraft.

It is 13 February 1604 and John Warne is owner of Snowshill. Related to him by marriage is Ann Parsons, an orphan of sixteen years of age who is heiress to her family's estate and living nearby at the home of her guardian Anthony Palmer. On that day Palmer, together with some of his friends and servants, forcibly took her from there to Snowshill Manor. There, in an upstairs room at midnight, Ann was married to Palmer by the vicar of Broadway.

Insisting she would not stop another moment in the manor house, Ann somehow managed to get the whole party to travel to the village of Chipping Campden, eight kilometres away, in the early hours of that morning. Even though the marriage was later dissolved by the Court of the Star Chamber it clearly must have made a deep impression on her.

Over the years there have been numerous reports of unexplained events in what has become known as Ann's Room. Footsteps have been heard crossing the empty room, a cold presence has been sensed, and a feeling of overwhelming sadness has unnerved a number of people.

SNOWSHILL ARMS

Sightings at this ancient inn have added to the number of recorded ghosts in the village.

Throughout the 1970s Alistair Biles was landlord of the Snowshill Arms. He is said to have frequently spotted a shadowy figure upstairs in the oldest part of the building. It would open doors and had also been seen to pass through walls. It appeared to be almost shapeless although there were times when this may have simply been the impression left by the ghost wearing a long cloak. None of the family ever felt threatened by the apparition, yet the dog would not remain settled when the figure was about. As soon as it could the family pet would take advantage of the recently opened doors and head downstairs to the public bars.

THE MONK

The lane running past the manor is the haunt of a monk. He appears as a shadowy presence, lurking around in the darker parts of the lane. Older residents of the village refused to walk around this part of the village after dark.

Some reports state he is from nearby Winchcombe Abbey, others maintain he was a moody monk who resided at the priory which stood on the same site as the current manor house.

SOUTH LEIGH

BALLASO BRIDGE

The name is a corruption of 'ballast hole', a quarry south of the railway line which is crossed by the bridge, and which supplied the stone for the construction of the railway.

In the 1870s this place witnessed the gruesome murder of Black Bess, who was killed by her boyfriend Charlie the Gyp and her body dumped in adjacent ballast hole. It is surprising to find the name not having taken on a reference to the horrors of the nineteenth century.

STANTON HARCOURT

LADY ALICE

It was in a room in a tower of Stanton Harcourt which now bears his name in which Alexander Pope worked on the translation of the *Odyssey* in 1718. During this time the village was the scene of a horrific murder story.

That day, Lady Alice Harcourt did not reach the church for the celebration of mass with the rest of her family. Whilst they were in the church literally a stone's throw away Lady Alice was in the tower, the victim of a murder made even more horrific by the way the poor woman's body was treated. Her lifeless form was cut to pieces and thrown through a small window to fall to the ground below.

That her restless spirit continued to walk the grounds for some time afterwards is hardly surprising. However, in the tradition of this region, her remains were removed and laid in one of the ponds. It was seemingly thought that such would put the ghost to rest. But no record of any success in this respect has ever been found, indeed were it not that this action was spectacularly unsuccessful we would likely be completely unaware of it.

A DRY POND

It should be said that other women's bodies were placed in these ponds. Although no record of the one haunting remains, it must be assumed that this was the reason an unknown woman was placed at the bottom of the pond. However, they failed to take into consideration the long dry English summers, for when the pond dries out she reappears, usually in a coach and four.

At nearby Manor Farm they were having problems with Mrs Hall. Her ghost was haunting the Harcourt Arms public house and the gardens of that establishment. She discovered her husband had been arranging secret liaisons with the landlady of the pub and was so distraught she committed suicide by taking poison.

As with the other women in Stanton Harcourt whose restless spirits could not find peace, she was reburied at the bottom of the pond. However, as soon as the pond dried out her presence would be noted once again.

STEEPLE ASTON

The Holt Hotel

There is a natural site for an inn at the crossroads of the road between Banbury and Oxford and that between Aylesbury and Chipping Norton, and there has been a sequence of stops here continuously for over 500 years. During that time a number of characters have quenched their thirst or satisfied their hunger under this roof, some of whom were revealed by the Haunting Breaks team who held the first of a series of events here towards the end of 2008.

These paranormal investigation evenings are to be held regularly. A conversation with Carol of Haunting Breaks revealed that during their first evening, the psychics reported much activity although much of it related to the guests on the night and as such is personal to them. However, one individual appeared to have been a resident memory of life at the Holt Hotel. Appearing to be a maid she was dressed in clothes which fitted with the nineteenth century and is said to have been seen in what had been the servants quarters. Thought to have been resident here, and with a rough approximation of the dates she was here, a little investigation failed to bring any potential employees to light.

However, the most famous apparition of the Holt is depicted on the sign outside. Highwayman Claude Du Vall is the resident apparition and has been reputedly spotted several times. He is a furtive shadowy figure in the passageways and on the stairs, while the sound of his galloping steed has been noted riding along the main road. As a ghost Du Vall is almost anonymous compared to the flamboyance of his criminal lifestyle. Born to the French aristocracy in 1643 he crossed the English Channel during the Restoration in the service of the Duke of Richmond. Twenty of so years later he was preying on travellers along the Oxford road, with his loyal henchman alongside him the victims were carefully chosen and most likely selected from visitors to the Holt where he was want to spend the proceeds from his illegal activities hereabouts.

It seems he took particular note of the fairest married ladies to pass through these doors, noting which way they were travelling and with whom. As the guests left he would make his way ahead of them and, along with his partner in crime, head them off further along the road. Here he would relieve the gentleman of his valuables and, accompanied by his colleague on the mandolin, would request a dance from his wife. If she consented she would be allowed to go on her way, a refusal meant she would also have her valuables removed from her person.

Du Vall was not averse to using the pistols he carried, taking the lives of unknown numbers. However, his stereotypical outfit, complete with black curly wig, black hat and matching mask, combined with his classic good looks and gallant manners, he was an irresistible magnet for the ladies. Indeed when his nefarious career came to an abrupt end with his arrest, several of these female admirers pleaded for his life. Yet their pleas fell on deaf ears.

Claude Du Vall was hanged at Tyburn in 1670, and the darkest chapter in the history of Steeple Aston came to a close.

STOW-ON-THE-WOLD

CHAPEN STREET

Whilst the rest of the nation was reeling from Beatlemania, the occupants of one house in Chapen Street had other things on their minds in 1963.

It started with pools of water spontaneously appearing around the house. Thinking it to be a plumbing problem workmen were called in to investigate. However, they could find no possible cause for the water problem, even though they witnessed the phenomenon themselves. Hauntings are generally to call attention to the individual, So, on reflection, the failure to recognise this as a ghost problem was probably unwise. The family would have realised this soon afterwards when things began to escalate.

This was no ordinary haunting, and turned out to be that most unpleasant of visitations – a poltergeist. Very soon furniture started being moved about. Heavy furniture suddenly jolted across a room, including one instance when the family's teenage boy was thrown from his bed. Apparently the poltergeist still did not feel he had got his message across and sheets were found ripped to shreds, deep cuts were found in a headboard, wallpaper was torn from the walls, writing thereafter appear on the plaster behind and, most disturbing of all, the hand of a child was seen which slowly grew into that of a man.

Now convinced he had the family's full attention, he chose to announce himself. A voice told them the problem was caused by a man who had been involved in the building of the house. Furthermore he had died twenty years previously on the very date the haunting had started. Being given a specific date made it easy to check and find that the man had indeed died on 15 February 1943.

Oddly enough the poltergeist seemed to consider himself at home. He was even said to have accompanied them on their annual holiday. While the problem itself never went away, he did tone down the haunting and the family learned to live with their visitor.

KINGS ARMS HOTEL

This grand old building graces one of the Cotswold's best-known villages. Since before the sixteenth century this former posting house has been one of the premier hostelries in Stow. Its most famous visitor was Charles I who stayed here on the night of 8 May 1645. It has, however, another longer term resident who has been sighted infrequently for at least the last century.

Following the Second Word War, the proprietor of the establishment seemed to enjoy a special rapport with the old lady who deigned to continue to use the hotel. She was dressed in black, maybe in mourning, her long grey hair tightly wound into a pile on top of her head. She never interacted with anyone specifically, yet she seemed fully aware of her surroundings. She is always seen in one room, the lounge, where a large television set is the modern focal point albeit surrounded by an assortment of furnishings and decor from at least one earlier age. Seated in a large armchair near the solitary window, she almost lauded over those who entered opposite through the sole door to the room, be they guests or staff.

The old woman appears to be aware of global warming and has been reducing the hotel's carbon footprint for at least the last fifty years by turning off the lights. Normally she does not create problems, but at times she can be a little over zealous and tends to switch off lights seconds after an individual has exited a room, even though they return almost straight away. She has also been known to be found by guests seated in her favourite chair in the lounge – particularly by those who were unaware of her antics – only to disappear the moment their back is turned. One visitor, after seeing her seated in her chair, described her as 'everyone's image of a maiden aunt' and yet shortly afterwards he discovered the bars on the electric fire in his room were on then off then on again. Doors that open and close of their own volition have also been blamed on the elderly woman

Who she is nobody knows, although it is suspected that owner of the hotel in the 1940s and 1950s may have been aware of her identity. Indeed the ladies may well have been related in some way for each may have worn identical pendants around their necks. Or are they the same one?

FOSSE WAY

On the highest point of this Roman road, just outside the town of Stow-on-the-Wold, two friends were treated to a glimpse from the past. It was 7 December 2004 and the two were travelling by car along the A429 in good light with excellent visibility, there were no distractions and each witnessed the same thing quite independently. As they cleared the brow of the hill they were suddenly confronted by a rather tall and imposing figure dressed in Victorian clothing and an old and battered top hat. So quickly were they upon him, although they were not speeding, that they narrowly missed running him over.

For the rest of that morning their conversation kept returning to the strange sight. Eventually they had convinced themselves that what they thought they had seen was not what they had actually seen. Their glimpse had been rather brief and, after all, they had almost run him down so they decided they were mistaken. That was fine until they were travelling home a few short hours later and were confronted by the same sight. However, this time they were in no danger of hitting him but were horrified to find the man simply disappeared in front of their eyes. The man's description was exactly the same as they had seen earlier that day and they were in no doubt this was the same man, or ghost!

ROYALIST HOTEL

Its claim as the oldest of England's inns is a strong one for there was an inn here in AD 949, and the number of reports of ghostly sightings is very high. For this information I am indebted to the owner of the establishment, Mark Vance.

Over the next thousand years the property has seen several uses. Initially founded as a leper hospital by the Saxon Duke Aethelmar, it was later taken over by the Hospitallers of St John for the same purpose. It was known as the Porch House, offered hospitality to the weary traveller as the Eagle and Child and was a combined workhouse and house of correction during the eighteenth century. In the nineteenth century it was two houses called Porch House and Holmlea, eventually becoming the Royalist Hotel we see today.

On a number of occasions, while work has been carried out in and around the building, some unexplained discoveries have revealed something of the history of the place. As with many old buildings this hotel is said to be host to a number of tunnels which served as escape routes for combatants during the English Civil War, the Dissolution of the Monasteries, the Gunpowder Plot and several other significant moments in English history. This equates to an enormous number of man-hours in digging out endless tunnels for just a few years of conflict.

Truth is, while there are undoubtedly some tunnel systems beneath the surface of the Cotswolds, these were created naturally by the action of water on limestone. The idea that every town and village of any age whatsoever has a honeycomb of escape routes beneath the ground is based more on folklore than fact, the little evidence uncovered more often reveals the site of a previously unknown cellar or dungeon. Unlike today it was easier to dig down and use the rock as natural walls rather than to build ever higher.

Other discoveries include the sixteenth-century Witches Circle next to the fireplace. This was common practice in these times to prevent these evil crones from gaining the access denied to them by closed doors and windows by descending the open chimney. As an added precaution salt boxes were kept by the fire so a pinch could be thrown on the flames to produce a flash and, so the story goes, would set fire to the skirts of the witch. Bowls of water placed by the fire would also prevent the witch coming down the chimney, for it was well known that witches would not cross water.

During the sixteenth and seventeenth centuries it was known as Porch House, the property of the Shellard family. It is the fourth generation of the family in this home we are particularly interested in, John Shellard who died on 13 November 1630 aged just fifteen. The family's time at the house was a turbulent one, political disagreements, trouble over religious beliefs, and in-fighting over inheritance made for anything but a quiet life for poor John. Again, the stories of the tunnels beneath Stow are heard as being the avenue for John's flight – even said by some to have been on horseback – where he is said to have met his end and was never seen again. It has been claimed that John was a messenger for the Royalists in and around Oxford. The exact date of his death was determined nine years after his disappearance by the inquest into the circumstances that surrounded the inheritance claimed by his brother, Thomas. It should be realised that the will and the inheritance were not finally agreed for over forty years, in 1681.

During the 1960s Tom Shellard, then present at the Royalist Hotel, saw an ominous and spooky figure on the staircase. The apparition was vague, the faint outline of a young man wearing high boots, a waisted coat and a bandoleer. Tom was convinced that what he saw was the image of his long-dead ancestor, the young John Shellard. Tom's explanation for his ancestor's appearance was said to be in order to make it known just how he had died and how.

According to one regular visitor, a clairvoyant, this is not the only ghostly visitor to the hotel. Notice the lady on the sofa in the bar and you will see her smiling and even talking to a host of ghostly visitors. The bar and restaurant is said to be alive with shadows, dogs and children playing, voices and laughter, and a great deal of merriment. She maintains a man died in the region between the bar and the reception desk, without a record of any death here is this a clue to the mysterious disappearance of John Shellard?

She also remarked on the sound of knocking in the early hours of the morning in one of the guest rooms, where two children wearing Victorian clothing have been seen. Some staff recalled how a couple who stayed in this room found these tapping sounds so unnerving that they left the hotel and spent the night in their car in the hotel's car park. Furthermore, outside room number two the clairvoyant detected a former lady of the house, said to be wearing a gorgeous long lace dress, while outside the door to number six a Cavalier in the most flamboyant of attire stands awaiting who knows what.

The medium says she can see two small girls in and around the building, they are always holding hands but there is a general impression from them of cold and loneliness. Lastly there is the mystery of the Black Knight. She is the only person ever to have seen this ghostly man in darkest of armour and, while it has been suggested this is a reminder of the days when the Knights Templar were around Stow, this particular order wore white.

Who sees what here appears quite selective. This however, is only to be expected as it seems that only certain individuals are tuned in to certain wavelengths and thus only experience some of what the Royalist Hotel apparently has to offer.

The Hartleys'

This eighteenth-century building was first used in 1763 as a rectory by the Hartleys and has stayed in the hands of that family for most of its 250 years history. Indeed, it was only 1901, when the long reign of Queen Victoria ended, that ownership changed. Yet by the 1950s the last rector to live here had bought the place back and, with ownership now back to the same Hartley family, it was soon to see its first years as a hotel.

The building lends itself well to guests, its many rooms had served as an emergency school for evacuees during the Second World War, and seemingly some are a little reluctant to leave. Particular problems have been sensed in room number eight, including one dramatic night when a guest awoke to find something he could not quite make out at the foot of the bed. He leapt from his bed in such a state of panic, that the adrenalin enabled him to tear a leg from the sideboard and begin thrashing wildly at the presence with the impromptu wooden club! It is not known if he was ever charged for the damage to the furniture. In more recent times another guest was preparing to go down to dinner when they heard and sensed something rushing around in the room. Although it seemed much longer the disturbance lasted a few brief seconds before diving underneath the bed, itself quite an achievement for there is no more than a two-inch gap underneath the divan.

A couple of years ago room number sixteen had a less vigorous but equally inexplicable occurrence. A married couple were staying at the hotel for a few days and he was alone in the room while his wife had popped out to the local shops. As he sat on the bed watching television he quite clearly felt someone sit down beside him. Thinking it was his wife back from her retail trip he turned to greet her, yet there was nobody there. However, there was a distinct dent in the quilt as if someone was sitting there. When she did return a few moments later she found her husband quite pale and subdued.

STROUD

A MAN IN BLACK

Today it is difficult for the younger generations to imagine a time when people were forced to walk to work, especially in more rural locations. Cars were a luxury item and bus services simply did not adequately serve many communities.

One such example was at Minchinhampton, where girls working at a factory in Chalford had no choice but to walk to and from work. This was not the greatest hardship during the balmy days of summer, but during the cold and dark winter nights the unlit roads after a hard day's work must have been dreaded. The one saving grace was there were a number of young women who had to make the same journey and, as there is safety in numbers, they would make the journey together.

It was on one of those cold, windy and rainy nights when the girls from the factory began the long walk up the hill toward home. Traffic was not a problem and so they linked arms across the road and bent their heads into the driving wind and rain. Their route always took them close by the Ragged Cot mentioned in the previous story. It was the young lady on the end nearest the old pub who first noticed the man in the field who seemed to be gliding a few inches above the grass in the field. Unconsciously, she began edging away from that side of the road and pushing into her workmates. This attracted their attention and they looked in the direction that she was pointing.

All reported the same thing: a man dressed in black, including a tall hat and cape, looking every inch the undertaker as he was carrying the small coffin of a child on his shoulder. This was enough to scare the line of ladies who promptly broke into the fastest run they could manage. None turned to look behind them, fearful of what they might see, and they did not stop until they reached the safety of their respective homes.

Was this the ghost of the undertaker, taking the body of the young child of Clavers who had so tragically died in the eighteenth century?

HORSELESS CARRIAGE

During the 1970s the area near the old Rodborough Manor on Rodborough Common was developed. The cutting of a new road and erection of plush new apartments in such an historic region should have been expected to bring about the odd sighting, which did infact occur.

Almost before the plaster was set and the gloss paint dry a couple were out walking one evening and watched in stunned silence as a horseless carriage passed them.

However, this was no early vehicle powered by an internal combustion engine, this was an old horse-drawn coach and four – but without the horses! Several other witnesses reported seeing the same thing heading along this newly developed road, while there have been further reports of a headless horseman galloping along here, while many have heard the sound of hooves galloping past yet neither horse nor rider can be seen.

MYSTERIOUS CYCLIST

Stroud Hill Road is not the easiest route for someone riding a bicycle. Ascending the hill would be a challenge for even the most accomplished athlete, while the descent would be a severe test for the brakes.

In those first years following the First World War, a man watched as a cyclist careered down the hill fighting to gain control of his bicycle. Upon reaching a right-hand bend he failed to change direction and continued on and over the hedge surrounding the field. He rushed to the man's aid but, despite a thorough search, could find neither the man nor his machine. A second man witnessed exactly the same course of events just four or five years later, yet, again there was no wreckage of a bike and no injured rider to be seen.

JAROLEN HOUSE

This was the former home of a wealthy businessman of Stroud who had a comfortable life with money derived from the textile industry. Little is known of the family, who kept to themselves and were not subjects of scandal or gossip.

It seems that the house and the employers were very attractive to one young lady who worked here during the nineteenth century. Dressed in a white apron over a long, flowing, grey dress, a maid has been seen on a number of occasions by drivers and pedestrians, seemingly still making her way to or from her beloved place of work.

As with many other eyewitness reports, the woman seems blissfully unaware of modern roads and buildings, traffic and people.

EDGE FARM

The name of the farm, itself taken from the hamlet, refers to its position on the edge of the Cotswold Hills. One field name here has been said to have the same basis, Hanging Hill Field being thought to come from it 'overhanging' the land beneath. This should not be taken literally, but simply as stating the place looms over the land below. Often such a name has attracted ominous and macabre definitions, as the author knows only too well from researching books on place names, yet this less glamorous definition is most often the real one. Ironically this case is quite the reverse.

During a discussion one evening a labourer was bragging of his prowess with the scythe. He boasted loud and long of how this particular field could be mown by him alone in but a single day. Remember he had no modern equipment, merely a scythe which he wielded by hand. Possibly much of his purported ability came from the bottle and his companions at the local inn had soon wagered heavily against him accomplishing such a formidable task. It will come as no surprise to find he failed and took his own life at the end of a noose.

Whether his suicide was due to embarrassment or because he could not afford to settle his losses, we shall never know. Yet Hanging Hill Field is now where the ghostly sound of the labourer can still be heard, an eerie swishing of the blade as he continues to cut down the ghostly stems as midnight approaches.

SWINDON

RATTLES TO RUSTLES

During the first half of the twentieth century the village proclaimed itself the most haunted in Gloucestershire. However, 'the most' is a difficult thing to quantify, do we count the number of different ghosts, the number of appearances, or is it expressed as a ratio of the total population of the place? A quote by Mark Twain sums this up quite well: 'Lies, damned lies, and statistics' which was also used for the title of Benjamin Disraeli's biography.

During Disraeli's political career his great rival was William Gladstone, whose grand-niece had a home in the village during the 1920s where she had a ghost with an even higher profile than her ancestor. Swindon Hall played host to Henry VIII and Anne Boleyn during their lifetimes, and their coats of arms adorned the hall for centuries afterwards. For many years stories of the king and queen quietly roaming the grounds and fields around the hall have filtered through. Within the old building Henry Tudor was much more vociferous, moaning and rattling chains, yet this may have been simply to attract attention for as soon as the owner of the hall called out 'Henry, go to bed!' the noisy monarch desisted.

In the grounds of the hall the descendants of Gladstone have, for as long as they have been in residence, set aside one small area as a pet cemetery. One grave was rather special to the lady who was here in the 1920s, for it was here her beloved Labrador,

Peter, was laid to rest. Apparently for many years this was the only spot in the entire village where bluebells bloomed each and every year.

Centuries after Henry VIII's time, a squire was in residence at the hall. Betrothed to the most beautiful young lady in the village he was as happy as he could ever have imagined. However, she jilted him before they ever reached the altar and his temper suffered greatly as a result. From that day forth he abhorred women. He had a large wall built all around his home thus avoiding any possibility of seeing any female passing by. The maids who were employed at the hall were under strict orders to stay out of the squire's sight, for should he ever be aware of their presence they would be sacked on the spot.

As with most large buildings of this era there is also a lodge associated with it. On the road passing the two has been heard a phantom coach galloping at full speed. No sighting has ever been reported, for it only puts in an appearance on moonless nights.

A mature couple were resident at the lodge in the 1950s. One evening the lady of the house thought she heard her husband coming home and went to the door to meet him. He was nowhere in sight but she could see a shadowy figure of a woman approaching the gates. Thinking it was one of the maids from the hall she stepped out to meet her but as soon as she reached the gates the shadowy figure disappeared. If that was not enough to scare the poor woman, a few seconds later the sound of the rustling silk of a long dress passed close by her, almost as if that same figure had carried on walking. No wonder the woman felt her hair stand on end!

CHAPTER 15

TETBURY

CHAVENAGE MANOR

A delightful house, which began life as an Augustinian priory in the fourteenth century. Two hundred years later, in 1564, after the house had been taken over by a number of different individuals, it became the property of Edward Stephens. Then began a major rebuilding programme that resulted in the place much as we see it today.

As the English Civil War came to an end Nathaniel Stephens, who had supported the Parliamentarians and had backed the call for the execution of Charles I, was living at Chavenage. His daughter Abigail, who may have been more than a little sympathetic with the reigning monarch, predicted that awful retribution would befall the family because of her father's political actions.

It seems her warnings were correct, for shortly afterwards Nathaniel fell ill and soon lay dying. As his final breath escaped his body outside the house a strange sight came into view. A horse-drawn coach of unparalleled splendour entered through the gates. It was driven by a headless coachman wearing quite resplendent attire adorned by the Star and Garter on his chest, insignia worn by only twenty-four people at any one time – including the king. Magically the door opened up without anyone touching the handle and, at the exact moment, the ghostly form of Nathaniel Stephens emerged from the house wrapped in his shroud. He boarded the coach and it pulled away, only to burst into flames and vanish as it reached the gates. It is said that since that time every Lord of the Manor has passed into the next world in exactly the same way.

The manor is also home to a small chapel. Without any sizeable congregation there is no need for resident clergy; however, there have been many reports over the years of a resident monk. The nearest monastery was built at nearby Horsley, where Augustinian Monks had settled in the first years of the House of Normandy. By the time of the reign of the Tudors, Henry VIII had broken from Rome and begun to close down the monasteries. Since this time there have been reports of a shadowy figure being seen in and around both house and chapel. This figure is that of a solitary monk, seen at prayer within the chapel and also approaching the place of worship when he is said to vanish when coming close to the building.

In all the history of the manor house, the chapel and the nearby priory the spectral monk is the only link between them. Maybe the spirit of this man of the cloth, robbed of his home by the Dissolution of the Monasteries, comes to the chapel as the only place that he could find to pray.

Chavenage House, near Tetbury. (Photograph courtesy Jeremy Clifton-Gould.)

CHAPTER 16

UPTON ST LEONARDS

THE CARPENTER

During the eighteenth or nineteenth centuries the local vicar was walking to work one morning. Of course, the vicarage was not far from the church and he had not far to go, indeed he had as far to walk through the churchyard as he did along the lanes. The man was quite new to the parish and would have recognised few, if any, of his parishioners.

To find someone walking in the grounds of the churchyard was not unusual, as friends and family would often go there to tend the graves of lost loved ones. However, there was something particularly odd about the man the parson saw that morning. For a start he was huge, a positive giant of a man who was impossible to miss. Furthermore he almost had the appearance of not being quite there. As the clergyman watched him he disappeared around the corner of the building, yet when the vicar followed he was nowhere to be seen.

Visibly shaken, the vicar told a colleague of what he had seen. The gravedigger recognised the description as that of Bill, the local carpenter. Later it emerged that Bill had been found dead that morning at the bottom of his own garden. Locals were well aware that marital relations between Bill and his wife were strained, to say the least, and she was instantly the prime suspect. However, no cause of death could be found, and it was presumed he had simply dropped down dead. Bill was given a decent Christian burial and the matter was forgotten for a generation.

Twenty years later the vicar had a very vivid dream and, when he awoke, hurried to the churchyard. Here he found the gravedigger once more and the vicar narrated what he had seen in his dream. Once again, he had seen the ghost of the carpenter, but this time the ghost had spoken to him saying that the next day there would be developments and the circumstances surrounding his death would be revealed. While the vicar entered the church the grave was dug ever deeper until he came upon a skull, a large skull which was obviously that of the giant carpenter.

Close examination revealed a brass pin embedded deep in the back of the skull. It had left no trace and when the body was first found x-ray technology was yet to be discovered, but stood out clearly now the flesh had fallen away. Immediately it was seen how he had died and his wife was the obvious culprit. Within hours she had fallen ill and she died shortly afterwards – but not before she confessed to the murder of her husband twenty years before.

CHAPTER 17

WESTON ON THE GREEN

WESTON MANOR HOTEL

This establishment has not always been a hostelry, indeed before the sixteenth century it was a monastery. Therefore it may seem odd that the ghost is not that of a monk but of a nun who is the subject of many a tale in the history of the village.

During the fifteenth century one young nun at a neighbouring retreat was repeatedly visiting the monastery, although not in any official capacity. Mad is the epithet applied to Maude, the nun who was apparently so insane she had forgotten her vow of chastity taken when she joined the order. It is said she was regularly escaping from the confines imposed by the sisterhood and making her way to the monastery where, in flagrant disregard of their religious beliefs, she engaged in pleasures of the flesh with several monks.

It appears the convent were, at first, somewhat tolerant of her indiscretions in view of her mental state and attempted to absolve her of her sins through prayer. Eventually though even the sisterhood appears to have lost patience and she was burned at the stake, although it is said that as the flames licked around her feet her madness left her and she begged, too late, for mercy. The sudden change of heart of the mother superior would almost certainly be due to pressure from the monastery, although significantly there is no record or story of any retribution or punishment of all, or any, of the monks. Maude is said to wander the streets around the hotel and has been seen in the grounds and skulking through the corridors and cellars of the hotel, her presence often said to be accompanied by chills and an eerie sensation. Perhaps Maude has been unable to find peace for two reasons: that her 'madness' was feigned, hence her sudden sanity when death stared her in the face at the stake, and also her anger at being held solely responsible for what had happened.

Maude is the best known but not the only apparition of the hotel. In the courtyard outside a phantom coach and horses can be heard hurtling across the ancient surface and around the old stables, while others have reported the ground shaking beneath their feet and shadows and chills have also been said to be a part of the experience. These chills and shadows may also be signs of the third apparition, that of a dairymaid who threw herself from the tower in a suicidal leap. One report, seemingly passed down since Victorian times, speaks of people hearing the screams of the young girl as she plummeted to her death. Thankfully this is the only time anyone has experienced this chilling sound.

WINCHCOMBE

THE MONKS OF WINCHCOMBE

The abbey has seen turbulent times since its founding in AD 798 by the Mercian King Kenulph. Within twenty-five years it was one of the largest and most prosperous religious communities in the country. Such a powerful establishment attracted the interest of those who would use it to realise their own aspirations.

The original building was severely damaged by a lightning strike in 1091. Rebuilt, it lasted for over four centuries until the Dissolution of the Monasteries by Henry VIII between 1536 and 1540. The only remains known to be from the abbey have been

Winchcombe's restored railway station.

moved to nearby Winchcombe church. Here two stone coffins, which are said to contain the remains of Kenulph and his son Kenelm, can still be seen. Virtually nothing of the abbey still exists today.

However, Henry VIII cannot possibly have considered the tenacity of the monks. Had he envisaged those of this religious order still being seen and heard in the twenty-first century, he may have thought twice about pulling down the abbey and relieving it of its treasures. Exactly where the abbey stood have been heard the hymns and chants of a ghostly choir, always around midnight. North of here, around the sight of the old railway station, is seen a shadowy figure appearing to be a monk in his robes, who would seem to be walking half a metre above the present ground level. Is it possible that this was the level of the land when the monks were still resident at Winchcombe Abbey?

This religious figure is not alone here. Indeed the region seems a positive hive of ghostly monks, one appearing at Pike Bank and another at Margaret's Hollow. This latter sighting caused a cyclist great consternation, for he blamed the apparition for causing his bicycle to seize up completely. In the dark he was unable to find a cause for the problem and was forced to pull it along the road. The next day he gave it a thorough inspection and still found no reason for the malfunction, in fact it was now working perfectly.

BELAS KNAP

A long barrow or burial mound which archaeologists have dated to around 1400 BC. Extensively excavated, thirty-eight skeletons were uncovered along with various artefacts now held in the church museum at Winchcombe. Among these remains were the bones of five children, aged between five months and eight years. Animal bones, including horses and dogs, were also found although these were not complete skeletons.

It is aligned in a north-south direction, measures fifty-two metres in length, is eighteen metres at its widest point and stands four metres high. As can be seen this was a major construction job over three millennia ago, using little more than hand tools, which has stood the test of time. Undoubtedly it is an important historical site today, yet during its long history it has held even greater significance.

During its long life it must have been witness to some remarkable changes. Perhaps one visitor to this historic site in the middle of the twentieth century glimpsed a memory from the long history of Belas Knap. Everyone who comes here spends a few moments drinking in the wonderful view afforded by its elevated position.

However, when one lady was gazing across the fields she noticed a group of monks making their way to where she was standing by the barrow. She withdrew for a few

Belas Knap, near Winchcombe.

moments, assuming the monks would appreciate a little privacy for whatever ritual they were there to perform at the sacred site. When the monks failed to reach the place she returned and was stunned to find the view had changed appreciably. Not only were the monks nowhere to be seen, but the grass was shorter, there were fewer trees and even the patchwork pattern of fields was completely different. Had her earlier view been a glimpse through a window in time, a time when life was much simpler?

One family had a most unsettling experience when they arrived to picnic on top of the restored burial mound. It was a lovely day: warm, perfectly calm and not a breeze stirred the leaves of the beech and oak. This was to be a sumptuous repast, enough food to feed a sizable family was set out alongside crockery, not paper or plastic but the traditional tableware and cutlery. Imagine their surprise then, as they sat themselves around the feast, to find the tablecloth suddenly tossed into the air and scattering people, tablecloth, food and containers in every direction. A few minutes later the family had packed away their belongings and had returned down the steep slope to their car.

The road that runs past the site has also produced some strange reports. A blue figure is said to step out into the road, seemingly oblivious of the traffic. It is interesting to note that the drivers speak of the individual being seen crossing both toward and away from the ancient mound. Despite the unsettling nature of having a person step out in front of your vehicle, these drivers' reports can be accepted as accurate. However, it does raise the question as to where this figure is heading to or from?

111

SUDELEY CASTLE

With royal links dating back to the twelfth century this delightful home has been sited as the home for a number of ghosts over the years. However, its most famous inhabitant, the sixth and last wife of Henry VIII, Catherine Parr, is not one of them.

The one ghost had always been associated with Prince Rupert of the Rhine, nephew of the King and his right-hand man during the English Civil War. The Royalist commander had made Sudeley his headquarters and returned here on many occasions during the hostilities, even having a room named in his honour. With the majority of Gloucestershire siding with the Parliamentarians the castle was under siege three times during this period. Rupert survived all three but his black dog was a casualty of the first engagement. Over the centuries the castle has had many reports of the ghostly black dog walking the grounds and also being spotted behind previously closed doors.

However, an occupant of the castle during the early years of the twentieth century maintained the dog was his and that a photograph of him with his favourite animal stood on the mantelpiece in one room. It was said that if the photograph were ever removed from its normal resting place, that a succession of woes and misfortunes would befall the ancient home. The photograph is not visible anywhere and, although the archivist has searched high and low for the picture for many years, it has never been found and it thought to be a myth.

Back in the castle there is, as already mentioned, a Rupert Room. This is the main haunt of Janet, although she has also been seen in the main bedroom and the sewing room. Janet eventually served as housekeeper here, part of her fifty years unbroken service. She is said to have lived at Rushley Lane, yet she most likely came from one of the farms on this lane and would have lived in the castle itself. She is usually seen as a younger woman, dressed as a maid with her mob cap, white blouse, a well-worn pink and white striped skirt reaching down to her black shoes.

Janet was a well-known character around Winchcombe, her love for the castle unquestioned and it assumed she would never have wanted to leave its employ; seemingly she soon returned.

GHOSTLY PHYTHIAN

When Sarah Bleby married John Phythian at the end of the eighteenth century she could never have dreamed of how her life, and that of her family, would develop. She was a wealthy woman, having inherited an estate near Tewkesbury. This was sold and aided her husband's purchase of various properties around Winchcombe where they had made their home. Phythian was a man of medicine, described as both a surgeon and an apothecary.

This well-liked couple had four children, of which all three sons sailed west to seek fame and fortune in the exciting new land of opportunity known as the Americas. Of particular interest to us here is the second son, Joseph Tyler Phythian, who became embroiled in the rebellion of the Panamanians against the ruling Spanish. He was captured by the Spanish and managed to escape; however, he was soon recaptured and shot in front of a firing squad.

Over 3,000 miles east of here in Winchcombe his mother awoke with a start. To her great distress she discovered the ghostly, bloodied form of her son standing beside her bed, and hence she learned of the death of her son many weeks before the official news filtered across the Atlantic.

CATHERINE PARR

The only one of Henry VIII's wives to survive him spent her last days at Sudeley Castle and was buried near there in 1548. A farmer by the name of John Lucas discovered the coffin towards the end of the eighteenth century. However, he had no idea what he had found until he opened it and discovered the perfectly preserved body of the queen, with further identification provided by the inscription therein.

Despite being severely chastised for desecrating the burial of the queen, Lucas and a number of his companions once again removed her from the resting place after a bout of particularly heavy drinking. None of those present at this time died a natural death, all found an untimely end to their lives in what was said to be quite horrible circumstances. As Lucas's death approached he suffered bouts of madness, thus Dr Phythian was sent for. In one of his more lucid moments he found the words to describe his horror at the appearance of the queen as he passed her grave one night.

As the stories of this haunting spread nobody dared to look inside the coffin again until 1817, when it was decided to remove it and give it a decent Christian burial once more. Dr Phythian examined the corpse and declared that her hair, by then known to continue to grow after the death of the individual, had now reached her feet. He snipped off a lock of her hair to add to his rather macabre collection but this was later burned by a descendant fearing it being used for purposes of witchcraft!

OLD WINCHCOMBE

In a village of old houses one of the most ancient properties provided a fright or two for a couple who had volunteered to look after both home and pets while their friends were away. At first their task was a joyous one: a warm summer and quintessential

English country garden surrounding a building which had Elizabethan foundations, and rebuilds in both the Jacobean and Georgian styles.

Despite the heat of the summer they were increasingly concerned by the cold which invaded their bodies within the house. Furthermore the electrics seemed to have a mind of their own: the lights and a radio which were certainly off when they left the house were on and working by the time they returned. A doorknob to the main bedroom was rattled, almost angrily, while the lounge door flew open without warning and caused an ornament to fall from the mantelpiece. In the kitchen there was no relief, saucepans swung from their hooks and a bag of knitting yarn was also known to move without apparent cause.

Yet the most convincing reason for believing they were not alone came one night shortly after they had retired to bed. The eerie atmosphere was most palpably unwelcoming and they had gone to bed early. Sleep did not come easily and they were awoken suddenly by the dogs barking madly downstairs and the bathroom taps which had suddenly decided it was the right time to gush forth at maximum rate. The man turned off the taps and settled the dogs but no sooner had they gone back to bed when the taps were flowing once more. Over the following three nights this pattern was repeated, the wife insisting she could also hear the rustling of papers.

A nun is said to have been seen in and around the building, sometimes said to be a nurse, while a young boy who once lived there asked his parents who the kindly lady was who had been chatting to him whilst seated on the side of his bed. Furthermore in the garden was a hermitage, said to have been occupied during the twelfth century, and tunnels leading from the cellars to Winchcombe Abbey.

WITHINGTON

MILL INN

In the latter half of the twentieth century a number of individuals witnessed a strange site in the pub. This old pub has a large fireplace, a pleasant focal point in the winter months.

It was around this fireplace that the same image has been seen. Three figures have been witnessed, described as shades or hazy silhouettes, standing in a line in front of the fireplace. It is impossible to say which way they are facing, as they are only outlines. On either side is a man, both tall and most likely dressed in late eighteenth or early nineteenth century attire. However, it is the figure between them that is the most interesting. A woman with an exceedingly large hat stands between the men – the hat being quite important for it fits the description of a former landlady who drowned in the nearby River Coln. The circumstances surrounding her death have never been fully clear. As soon as they are noticed the three fade from view, none of them having moved a muscle.

This was the scene of intense activity some years ago when a former landlord and his family all witnessed bottles, glasses, cutlery and kitchen equipment moving of their own volition. However, this could not be explained as being caused by a breeze, in order for the objects to have reacted as they did it would have been a very strong gale blowing through the place and yet all was calm.

WITNEY

GRAMMAR SCHOOL

The grammar school was founded in the seventeenth century by Henry Box and completed in 1660, two years before his death. The ghost is said to be found in the school's library. He does not actually interact with the modern world – indeed he seems totally unaware of it. Yet his appearance to a cleaner in the library was enough to ensure that she refused to clean that particular part of the building on her own thereafter. Henry Box has a memorial in the parish church, it was organised and paid for by his widow Mary.

WOODCHESTER

WOODCHESTER PARK

Not all hauntings are already consigned to history, some can be considered contemporary. Such as the film crew that, at the beginning of the twenty-first century, were spending the night at the mansion.

The house was designed by Benjamin Bucknall and built from local Cotswold limestone. Based on the French Gothic style, work continued for sixteen long years and, in 1870, workers gave up with much of the seventy-nine planned rooms still unfinished. This has resulted in a strange collection of tools and gargoyles strewn around the place, while corridors and doorways lead nowhere.

For a quiet corner of the Cotswolds it has a number of ghosts dating from a variety of periods throughout history. The most modern ghost was heard, perhaps for the first time, by the film crew who were staying here overnight. They were suddenly aware of a strange and persistent banging which approached them becoming progressively louder. Eventually they realised this was no hammering they were hearing, for it climaxed in the unmistakeable cacophony of a steam railway locomotive working at its hardest. This is rather hard to explain as the railway is over a mile away at its closest point.

It has been claimed that there are no less than sixteen quite distinct hauntings around this estate at Woodchester. As the house itself was never finished and therefore largely uninhabited the vast majority, including that of the steam train, are within the grounds. The most obvious feature of the valley through the estate is the chain of small lakes. Largely a natural feature, when seen from the ideal viewpoint the water reflects the light in the sky like a row of jewels. It is seen at its best on a clear moonlit night and must have proved an irresistible magnet for one young Dominican monk one rather cold winter.

Known as the Novice of Woodchester he is said to walk the lovely grounds around the lakes. Perhaps he is reflecting on how he should have stayed on solid ground that winter day when his young life came to a tragic end. During a time when the winter chill had capped every lake with a sheet of ice, the monk went skating. Yet he should have been more cautious, for the ice was not as thick as he had thought and could not support his weight. He drowned in the freezing waters and was found when the ice thawed.

Almost none of the ghosts here can be considered contemporary to the present building. To the south of the estate, a Roman soldier has been seen patrolling the area near the gates, an entry point which did not exist until centuries after the last remnants of the great empire had vanished, so what he is guarding is unknown. At another gate serving the mansion house a phantom coach and four has been witnessed pulling both in and out through the gates, only to slowly fade from view as it gets further away from the gates themselves.

The estate also seems to be a draw for ghostly horses and their owners. In the centre of the fifth lake is a small island. On here a headless horseman has been seen riding round and round the perimeter and always in an anti-clockwise direction. Presumably trapped by the rising waters when the estate was first landscaped, maybe the secret to his escape is simply to reverse the direction of his endless circuits of the island. Along the drive a horse and rider, whose clothing identifies him as a seventeenth-century nobleman, has been seen and heard trotting leisurely along the ancient path.

There have been several impressive houses built here over the centuries. The present building was begun by William Leigh, a nineteenth-century gentleman who had recently been converted to Catholicism. He built the priory and had started the house seen here when he ran out of money. Prior to this the earlier eighteenth-century mansion was the home of the Dulcie family, the gates of the estate are all that survive from this era. Before this it had been home to Thomas Arundel. At the time of the Reformation it was not safe to be a practising Catholic, as Arundel found when he was executed for refusing to renounce his faith. He continues to wander the estate, a sad and lonely spectre.

Other reports include that of a black dog, a dwarf, a coffin floating over the waters of one of the lakes, and a headless Roman. During the Second World War American troops were barracked near here, which explains why the ghosts of two of them were seen smoking cigarettes as they roamed through the parkland. It was used for training exercises by the soldiers who saw tragedy strike in the spring of 1944. A pontoon had been built and was being crossed by several armoured vehicles when it collapsed under the weight. Several servicemen died on the spot directly beneath where two of their colleagues had seen an angel surrounded by a glowing white aura hovering moments earlier.

Paranormal investigators camped out all night to witness a bell ringing from a tower where no bell is hung, the hands of a broken clock moving, and those in the group having long hair reporting it being tugged, and the next day the lights in the building came on when nobody but the caretaker was present.

WOODSTOCK

BEAR INN

This twelfth-century establishment is in the town known as the Gateway to Cotswolds. Of course, whether this is a gateway or not depends entirely upon which direction it is approached from.

Not only is this a charming pub and eating-house but it also has accommodation available upstairs. During filming nearby in 1967 some of the cast and crew stayed at the Bear with very differing degrees of success. Room sixteen seemed to be the haunted room, a place where visitors discovered several of their personal belongings had been moved, never taken but simply relocated nearby.

Many others had heard the sounds of footsteps walking across the boards at night, highly polished wooden flooring creaking under the weight of the unseen individual. The noises had woken one member of the film crew who had demanded a change of room. Even though it was an actress that volunteered to swap hotel rooms he felt no embarrassment and looked forward to a night's rest. However, the next night in room sixteen the young lady was awoken by the sound of footsteps and opened her eyes to find a lamp across the room had been switched on. At breakfast the following morning the actress reported the events to the duty manager. He informed her that this was the fourth time he had heard about strange events in that very room in the short time he had been working at the place.

Shortly afterwards the entire place was redecorated and no further activity in room sixteen was reported. However, after work was completed here at the beginning of the twenty-first century the movement of objects seems to have started again.

BLENHEIM PALACE

This is the country seat of the dukes of Marlborough and is considered one of the finest examples of baroque architecture in England. It is named after the Battle of Blenheim, the conflict of 1704 when John Churchill masterminded the defeat of the French armies of Louis XIV, and was a gift of land and monies from Queen Anne in recognition of this pivotal victory.

What resulted was the present palace, which has been described as more of a royal and national monument rather than a home. However, for 300 years it has been one of the most sumptuous of England's homes. It was the brainchild of architect John Vanbrugh, whose selection was rather surprising for he had little experience of design. Indeed he had been a soldier, was considered an expert in military espionage, and was best known as the author of a number of comedies. Yet the Duke was impressed by his contributions to the building of Castle Howard in Yorkshire and he was invited to begin.

However, work did not proceed smoothly: disagreements between the queen and the duchess, lack of money, disgruntled masons and continual stoppages resulted in Vanbrugh being dismissed. When he next attempted to come back and complete the work he was refused entry to the park by the duchess. It seems she was the centre of most conflict in the days of the first duke at the palace, and one story concerned her attempting to marry off her granddaughter to Frederick, Duke of Wales with the promise of a substantial dowry of £100,000. The granddaughter, who was the then Lady Diana Spencer, never wed the Duke of Wales despite the financial incentive.

Another individual seemingly displeased with the duchess has continued to make his annoyance known. In the days of the first duke he had his own chaplain living at the palace. Dean Jones is said to haunt the room in which he resided, apparently searching for a book he loaned the duchess. Some stories describe Jones as 'the black ghost' yet this is probably from the picture of him in another room where he is wearing the black attire of a cleric.

Former Prime Minister Sir Winston Churchill was born in this very room. He arrived rather abruptly one evening while the palace was host to one of its extravagant parties thrown during the Victoria era. He is said to have joked that his appearance there had exorcised the ghost of Dean Jones once and for all. Yet this seems to be wishful thinking for there is a written record of a sighting after Sir Winston's birth in 1874.

In her memoirs, published under the title of *The Glitter and the Gold*, Consuela Vanderbilt told the story of how she went from becoming a daughter of one of the most influential and wealthy families in America to becoming the wife of the 9th Duke of Marlborough and her new life across the Atlantic. As the couple did not marry until 1895, and she had never been to Blenheim Palace before 1896, the following narrative shows the ghost was still reported over twenty years after Sir Winston's arrival.

Although no date is mentioned, the duchess states she had invited a young female friend to stay as her guest at the palace. She had been given the very room which had first been that of chaplain and later the birthplace of the future prime minister. The book tells of how she awoke in the night to find the ghost of Dean Jones looming over her. The resulting screams awoke much of the household and she refused to spend another second in that room.

As Consuelo did not come to the Cotswolds before 1896 this seems to have disproved Sir Winston's exorcism claims. However, around this period Churchill was working in South Africa as a journalist reporting on the Boer War. Indeed he famously was captured by the enemy and yet managed to escape and find his way to friendly territory unaided. Thus it is possible he simply never heard of the events back at his family home in Oxfordshire.

WOTTON UNDER EDGE

RAM INN

The former Ram Inn is now a private house. Recently, the owner was forced to close as a licensed premises because of the cold. Paranormal researchers have been investigating the long-standing story of the resident ghost. The licensee cited the researchers as being the catalyst for the escalation in events, which have been increasingly less peaceful.

The property has parts dating from at least the twelfth century. It is a listed building and, as such, there is a limit to the amount of work that can be carried out. Central heating cannot be used to fend off the cold spots as there is a danger of warping the timber framework. The owner insists the freezing cold spots have worsened since the investigations began, making life in his own home almost intolerable.

It used to be little more than a nuisance, although some may consider being thrown across the room, being rocked in a chair, and pushed from behind on the stairs rather more than a nuisance. However, the place was already known as a possible ghost haunt when it was bought in the late sixties. It had been empty for three years and was heading for likely demolition. Eight centuries of history have brought about many stories, including several murders and inexplicable fatalities, exorcisms and devil worship. How many are fact and how many are fiction is unclear. However, there is some justification for thinking the place is haunted by at least one presence.

Lights have been seen flickering for no apparent reason, while the electrics elsewhere are completely unaffected. Upstairs in the so-called 'Bishop's Room', female guests who have slept there have complained of feeling cold hands upon their person. There are also reports of a dark form and of invisible hands felt running up their legs from the ankles in an eerie caress.

Over the years stories have been passed down of some quite eerie sightings, including black cats, monks, witches and a Cavalier. On one occasion a puddle of water inexplicably appeared on the wooden flooring. Tradition had it that this was where a woman known as the Blue Lady was buried by her murderer, to hide the body. It seems that when one leaned over and peered into the puddle the reflection staring back was that of the murder victim.

Indeed the Blue Lady is the most often reported ghost at the Ram Inn. This woman is described as a beautiful woman in her thirties wearing a long, blue cape with a hood and seen to glide, rather than walk, through the place. Her identity is a mystery, and although the name of Elizabeth has been quoted this may have been given to her after her death. No record of a murder to fit the evidence exists. Does this mean the perpetrator of the crime was never caught, or maybe even that the crime was never discovered? Furthermore this woman would surely have been known to someone, and seems to have been from a prosperous background, so it does seem surprising that her disappearance is not recorded. It could well be that we are looking in the wrong place and the Blue Lady was just a visitor to Wotton-under-Edge.

There are suggestions that the building was constructed on the site of a former burial pit. However, this story could have been created to fit in with the ghostly appearances, and there is no archaeological evidence of any burials at this location.

KINGSWOOD HOUSE

This home has seen more than its fair share of ghostly phenomena. Although none seem in any way frightening, they do hold some surprises even considering they are ghost stories.

The length and breadth of the country holds stories of a ghostly coach and four trotting or galloping along between stops. It is rare indeed to find any mention of them cornering, for this is one of the most difficult manoeuvres. Thus finding a coach and four here reputed to enter through the main gate and trot along to, and around, the house before retracing its path along the drive and back out of the gates, where it promptly fades from sight, is a refreshing and unusual change.

The Ram Inn, Wotton under Edge.

The Ram Inn, a place not afraid to
advertise its ghosts.

Another common ghostly sight is that of a black dog. Here the animal is said to emerge from behind the house and disappear across the field directly opposite the house. Ghostly black dogs are often a harbinger of doom, which are among the worst of omens. However, in this case there are no tales of foreboding associated with the creature, so perhaps this time the hound is simply a pet. Yet surely it cannot be the pet of the Grey Lady, for she approaches from along the road to Kingswood itself, through the gate and up to and into the house.

All of these reports have nothing in common, except perhaps the date for the carriage and the lady seem to be contemporary. Of course, it is impossible to date the appearances of the dog.

NEWARK PARK

The original building was completed in 1550, a four-storey Tudor design built for Sir Nicholas Poyntz. Remodelled in 1790 by architect James Wyatt for the Clutterbuck family, it was presented to National Trust in 1949 by Mrs Power-Clutterbuck.

Sir Nicholas was granted Kingswood Abbey at the time of the Dissolution of the Monasteries, hence why it is suggested that the monks have returned to haunt this building. Beneath the abbey were escape tunnels, although most were false and only one led to safety. However, the monks failed in their attempt and were sealed in their own makeshift tomb where their bones still lie today. However, on the Eve of All Saints' Day their spirits would issue forth from the panelled wall in the main room and be seen descending the large staircase. The candles they carried flickered at every step and they sang their plainchant chorus as they went through the building.

The stories from the house provided details of as classic a haunting as was to be found anywhere in the Cotswolds. Aside from the monks and their eerie chants, the rustling of a long and voluminous silk dress could be heard shuffling past as it, and its owner, journeyed from room to room almost drowning out the traditional bumps, bangs and rattles, while the feeling of brief but intense cold accompanied every experience.

Whilst tradition maintains the ghostly monks only emerge at the end of October each year, visitors to the house were more numerous in the spring and summer months in times past, just as they are today. Thus most versions of the tale must logically come from other times of the year, and documented reports would suggest the Hallowe'en-tide reference is one of fancy and for effect, rather than factual.

SYMN LANE

A murder victim of the late nineteenth century has proven a most disturbing image in this part of Wotton under Edge. She was an elderly woman whose delight at seeing her son again when he returned from Australia soon turned to dismay when she found out the reason for his return. The man had returned to claim his inheritance, somewhat prematurely as it turned out, which made him greatly displeased. In a fit of rage he killed the poor woman, effectively disinheriting himself at a stroke, then attempted to cover the evidence by setting fire to the cottage. He fled to Wotton Hill and was watching it burn when he was arrested.

Since that time the poor woman's spirit has been unable to find peace. Seen running screaming down the road where she died, her hair in flames and a look of terror on her face, she is enough to send a shiver along the spine of the bravest of souls.

WILL CREW

Many of the larger villages around the country have a local folk hero. A rogue, a rapscallion, a man who thought himself above the law but never did any real harm – a latter-day Robin Hood. Will Crew was just such a chap around Wotton under Edge, a man whose legend will continue to evolve as the years pass.

Between the wars, children of the village, who had to amuse themselves without the aid of television, were known to run around the churchyard where Will was laid to rest. The innocence of youth brings a bravado which we may not see in later life. Thus it was sheer devilment which saw them running through the churchyard and daring his ghost to rise and scare them.

Perhaps the children never discovered that Will Crew's ghost was said to have risen, and therefore did not fear any potential repercussions to their taunting. This was maybe because Will was spotted riding around Alderley to the south. It does call into question the validity of the report for he was said to have been seen without a head – which begs the question how was he recognised?

CHAPTER 18

YARNTON

SIGNAL BOX

The signal box at Yarnton Junction was once the talk of the railway workers around here. It seems it was haunted by a former signalman who worked here at the turn of the nineteenth century. Although he has never been seen it is easy to recognise him from his heavy footsteps across the floorboards. He pays no heed to anyone, nor has ever been said to be in any way threatening. It seems a pity he has earned the somewhat ominous sounding name of The Treader.

CHAPTER 19

A FINAL THOUGHT

In the preparation of this book the author consulted old newspapers, books and magazines. Appeals were made in the press, online and on the radio for personal experiences and family narratives. Indeed it was jokingly mentioned on air that should there be any ghosts listening an interview, without a Ouija Board or seance, would be most welcome. Dozens of individuals were spoken to who came from every walk of life. As stated in the introduction the author has yet to be convinced of the existence of ghosts and retains an open mind on the subject. However, one telephone call has certainly given him time for greater thought than any other story or lead. That it cannot be included under its location is simply that the narrator insisted that any names would have to be fictional and the name of the place must never be quoted.

Some years ago an army colonel returned from India. The days of British rule were coming to an end and the nation was about to be declared fully independent. As history records there was internal unrest too, leading eventually to the creation of the nation of Pakistan, and British personnel left a little more abruptly than they would have expected.

On arriving back in England he set about handling his affairs. Aside from a few years training and the time as a young boy growing up, he had not spent much time in England and was not looking forward to his new life with any particular enthusiasm. The colonel had had no immediate family as his parents had died many years before and he had no siblings. Indeed, his sole relation was an uncle, who, as he was to discover, had died on the first anniversary of VE-Day and left him as the sole beneficiary in his will. Not that the colonel needed the money, he already had a generous pension and had saved a nice little nest egg during his long years of service, but he now had a place to live, at least in the short term.

He took the train to the village, where the stationmaster directed him to the village pub. A short conversation with the proprietor resulted in a lift from a farmer, and moments later he was standing outside the wrought iron gates as the sound of the farmer's vehicle faded into the distance. First impressions mean a lot and, if this was to be his new home, he would have few complaints so far. The watery early afternoon sun made the local Cotswold stone walls of the building positively glow in welcome. The main gates were locked, but he gained entry via an open side gate and made his way to the front door.

His uncle's legal representative had informed him there were two employees still tending the place since the death of the late owner. Answering his knock a woman, whom he knew to be the cook and housekeeper, opened the door. Her husband tended the gardens and did other odd jobs. Here his first impressions were much less favourable for the woman was less than friendly, and almost surly in her greeting. The colonel made a mental note to seek out his former batman to offer him the position of manservant, even if he decided to sell the place. What little he learned from the ensuing conversation left him certain that this woman's employment was nearing an end.

The couple had their own home and did not live-in as had been suggested, indeed they both refused to venture anywhere near the place outside the hours of darkness. She would prepare his evening meal and leave it in the kitchen, returning next morning to cook breakfast and perform her duties. A brief tour of the house followed and she helped him unpack. He had chosen the bedroom which overlooked the village and, following a brief stroll around the grounds, headed off to the village to acquaint himself with the area.

Returning to the local pub, he introduced himself and made a few enquiries as to the history of the place and about his uncle. It was here he learned how the present building occupied the site of an old Dominican friary, destroyed as part of the Dissolution of the Monasteries. His uncle, a man who had shared his own military background, had rarely ventured far from his home. Increasingly suffering the debilitating pain of gout he was virtually house-ridden by the time of his death. The colonel warmed to these people despite their distrustful viwe of strangers. These communities rarely saw anyone new and this was of no consequence for he was not sure if he expected to stay or indeed if he would ever return.

He walked back the few hundred yards to the house. It was already dark by the time he left the pub, the moon providing adequate lighting and making the silhouette of the building a quite impressive sight. Entering through the back door he saw the meal ready as promised and, finding he was hungrier than he had realised, ate heartily. The rear entrance brought him through the house and to the main stone-floored hallway with its high, glazed, domed ceiling casting moonshine in a rainbow across the floor. Flicking on the light, he thought he heard someone and called out and searched but, when there was no sign of anything, decided it must have been an echo. A decanter provided a large scotch which he took with him to bed, intending to read.

For some reason he fell asleep quite early, waking as a clock struck an unknown hour. Confused at first, not knowing where he was and thinking there were – an absurd idea

– doves fluttering around the room, he went to the window and tried to wake himself fully. Below, walking along the same road he had taken himself, were a row of monks. Head bowed they passed right through the locked gates and continued around the estate, their white robes making them stand out clearly in the moonlight. Just then he heard a sound from outside his room, as if someone was climbing the stairs. Thinking he had been the target of a practical joke he opened the door to see a cloud of white doves fluttering upwards towards the coloured glass of the dome, their wings making no sound.

The next morning he questioned the housekeeper when she brought his breakfast. However, she was no more helpful than before, simply reiterating she had never been in the house after dark, never mind overnight. The local clergyman provided the answer a few days later. It seems the monks were an annual sight, appearing on the same three consecutive nights each year along with the doves. The staircase occupied the position of the chapel, where the monks were at prayer on the day their friary was set alight by the king's men. Their appearance is said to be a memory of that last journey that they took centuries before, while doves were popularly kept as a source of food at that time. Indeed the man pointed out a number of the remnants of these dovecotes, which were still visible in the walls of the outbuildings.

The colonel spent the rest of his life in the house. All, that is, save for three consecutive nights each year when he took a little trip and lodged at the hotel in the village. The name of the narrator was never revealed. The place was never identified and no attempt was made to discover the location of the place in question, out of respect for the gentleman's requests. In truth there is no proof that the story even belongs in a book on the Cotswolds, as it could have been set anywhere. Yet there is no reason to consider the lead a hoax any more than any other narrative.

It strikes the author that any story could be considered a work of fiction, for all reports come through a third party and there is no actual proof. Thus, none of these stories are told from the author's perspective, that will not happen until the day comes when the ghosts themselves agree to be interviewed directly. Unless that day already came when this final, anonymous story was told?

BIBLIOGRAPHY

Ghosts and Witches of the Cotswolds, J.A. Brooks
The A-Z of British Ghosts, Peter Underwood
The Ghosts Who's Who, Jack Hallam
Haunted Cheltenham, W.L. Cox and R.D. Meredith
Cheltenham Town of Shadows, Bob Meredith
The Ghosts of Gloucestershire, Keith Clark
Folklore and Mysteries of the Cotswolds, Mark Turner
Stroud News & Journal
Folklore of Gloucestershire, Roy Palmer